Contents

NNE FOXTON JB

GW00890460

Acknowledgements

This book developed from courses run with the TUC Education Department for union officials. I would like to thank the trade unionists – too numerous to mention – who attended these courses, for their stimulation and encouragement. I would also like to express my gratitude to the following, all of whom helped immensely in one way or another: Joyce Brown; John Connell; Michael Kidron; Mary Knowles; Richard Kuper; Jeremy McMullen; Judith Martin; Jim Mowatt; Paul O'Higgins; the staff of the English, Welsh and Scottish Industrial Tribunals and the Employment Appeal Tribunal.

Abbreviations

ACAS	Advisory Conciliation and Arbitration Service
AER	All England Law Reports
CA	Court of Appeal
CBI	Confederation of British Industry
CO	Conciliation Officer
COIT	Central Office of Industrial Tribunals
CRE	Commission for Racial Equality
DE	Department of Employment
DHSS	Department of Health and Social Security
EA 80	Employment Act 1980
EA 82	Employment Act 1982
EAT	Employment Appeal Tribunal
EOC	Equal Opportunities Commission
EPA	Employment Protection Act 1975
EP(C)A	Employment Protection (Consolidation) Act 1978
HC	High Court
HL	House of Lords
HMSO	Her Majesty's Stationery Office
ICR	Industrial Cases Reports
IDS	Incomes Data Services
IRLR	Industrial Relations Law Reports
IT	Industrial Tribunal
ITR	Industrial Tribunal Reports
IRLIB	Industrial Relations Legal Information Bulletin
NIRC	National Industrial Relations Court
QBD	Queens Bench Division of High Court
RRA	Race Relations Act 1976
ROIT	Regional Office of Industrial Tribunals
SDA	Sex Discrimination Act 1975
SI	Statutory Instrument
TUC	Trades Union Congress
WLR	Weekly Law Reports

1.

Introduction

What this book is about

Industrial tribunals – the best thing since Boddington's Bitter or the equivalent of a pint of Swarfega and a warfarin chaser? Both views are held in the labour movement. The view embodied in this book is that industrial tribunals *are a danger* to strong trade unionism *unless* we understand their real nature.

Industrial tribunals have nothing to do with the decision as to whether or not a worker is victimised or made redundant. These issues are resolved by the balance of forces between trade unions and employers. Tribunals can only set a price on what is an accomplished fact and even then only within certain limits. The fight for trade union rights has to be carried on at the bargaining table and on the picket line, not in the tribunal rooms. However, if you have *exhausted all trade union methods* to influence the decision at issue, understanding that tribunal remedies are second best, then there is nothing wrong with ensuring that compensation is as high as possible.

Sometime in their lives, most union members, shop stewards and full-time officials will be involved with an industrial tribunal case. The basic purpose of this book is therefore to ensure that, if a union member does end up in the second-best legal situation, he or she gets the most out of it. It is written basically for union activists who represent, help or advise members taking up tribunal cases and members who are involved in taking such cases themselves. Many activists know little about basic tribunal procedures, spend little time preparing their case, are overawed at the hearing, or leave far too much to the chairperson. Some tribunal cases are heard very informally, others are extremely formal. However, *all* tribunals operate by certain basic rules. The more you know the ropes, the better your chance of success.

If you are an effective union activist, you do not rely on outsiders in other circumstances. If you leave it all to the chairperson at a tribunal hearing, you may not maximise the full potential of your case and end up out of pocket.

This book attempts to explain in detail the basic rules of tribunal procedure as simply as possible and taking little for granted. (If you do want to find out more about the **substance** of the law on redundancy payments, unfair dismissal or other workers' rights, you must consult another book in this series, *Rights at Work* by Jeremy McMullen; it is only touched on here.)

It deals only with the situation where workers are trying to enforce *their* rights in a tribunal. It does not, for example, deal with the situation under the Tory anti-union legislation where workers and unions may be taken before a tribunal for, say, defending a closed shop. TUC policy is that union representatives should not sit on tribunals hearing these cases and trade unionists would be well advised to boycott such hearings. Neither does it deal with situations where employers are taken before a tribunal, such as appeals against notices under the Health and Safety at Work Act.

How to use it

Because you may well be using the law on tribunal procedure, I have tried to quote details of cases rather than just referring you to the Law Reports. If a case is vital to you you will, of course, want to read the actual report (see Chapter 7). Legal cases are cited in a particular way: *A. Anderson v British Olivetti Ltd* 1976 IRLR 287 means that Anderson was taking legal action in an industrial tribunal against his employer British Olivetti. This case is fully reported in the Industrial Relations Law Reports series for 1976 at page 287. *White v University of Manchester* 1976 IRLR EAT means that White was taking legal action against her former employers, Manchester University, and that having lost her case at the industrial tribunal she then appealed to the Employment Appeal Tribunal. Law Reports are usually produced weekly or monthly, and the pages are numbered consecutively over the whole year. At the end of the citation is the name of the court in initials – EAT, CA (Court of Appeal) or HL (House of Lords). Where there is no reference at the end of the case citation that case is an industrial tribunal decision. As you will see, it is the decision of the higher bodies that will help you most. Remember also that, because British law is constantly changing (see Chapter 2), some decisions may contradict each other. **As well as looking to the decision of the higher court, always look for the more modern decision, too.** The law is not only continuously changing and developing; it is often doing so in a way that is not logical or consistent. Sometimes there are no answers to a particular problem you may have. Sometimes the answers may be blurred. However, to the extent answers have been given by the tribunals and courts, you will find details here.

This volume is a handbook and intended to be detailed, so it is unlikely you will want to read it through at one sitting or even use all of it with one particular case. The idea is that you should pick out what is relevant to your own problem, or the stage of your case that you have reached.

The book is written in a rather artificial way. It assumes that you suddenly decide, 'we must go to a tribunal', and it traces the process through from there. Whilst the sequence followed here is a logical one, life is rather messier and you may in reality be involved in several of the processes described at the same time. For example, as soon as you decide that you wish to take a tribunal case, it would be wise to look at Chapter 11 on costs to see if the type of examples given there are likely to cause problems. You will want to use the information in Chapter 13 to prepare your compensation case as early as possible, not after the tribunal decision. When you are filling in an IT1 (Chapter 5), you may also find it useful to use the methods of strengthening your case described in Chapter 8.

To make it easier for you to see what each chapter covers there is a brief outline at the start and, if you are thinking of taking a case, it is important to glance through all these first.

The procedure of industrial tribunals is governed by *The Industrial Tribunals (Rules of Procedure) Regulations* 1980 (SI 884) which form the basis of this book. The equivalent provisions for Scotland (SI 885) and the Six Counties (1981, SI 188) however are now almost identical to those governing procedures in England and Wales. You are referred to two studies which give you a detailed account of tribunals in these two areas at the back of this book.

The legal position stated here is as it existed on 1 January 1983.

2.

Industrial tribunals and the legal system

If you are a worker or a representative deciding whether or not a case should be taken to an industrial tribunal, it is important that you should know how these tribunals work. In this chapter we look at the nuts and bolts of industrial tribunals:

- how tribunals developed;
- who sits in tribunals;
- how they are related to other legal bodies;
- the wider legal system; and
- the advantages and disadvantages of industrial tribunals for trade unionists.

If you want to get down to preparing a case straightaway then you can turn to Chapter 3. However, the information here will be useful in highlighting some of the problems that you may encounter later.

How tribunals developed

Industrial tribunals were first established in 1964 to deal with disputes over the payment of levies under the Industrial Training Act.

When the Redundancy Payments Act was introduced in 1965, tribunals were given the power to settle disputes over a worker's entitlement to a redundancy payment. The government also put complaints that workers had not received adequate particulars of their terms and conditions of employment under the tribunals' jurisdiction. The Donovan Commission in 1968 recommended that the jurisdiction of tribunals should be extended to cover all individual disputes between employers and workers stemming from their contracts of employment. They also felt that the industrial tribunals were suitable bodies to settle individual employment disputes and described the tribunals as providing,

a procedure which is easily accessible, informal, speedy and inexpensive and which gives employers and employees the best possible opportunities of arriving at an amicable settlement of their differences.

The 1971 Industrial Relations Act created more rights, such as unfair dismissal, which were to be dealt with by industrial tribunals. Whilst the TUC called on members of affiliated trade unions not to sit on industrial tribunals, there was no such boycott as far as taking cases to tribunals was concerned. Business doubled and when the 1974 Labour government replaced the Tory Act with an extensive set of new employment laws, the tribunals had finally arrived as the most important industrial relations courts, dealing with cases arising from over two dozen different legal rights.

Who sits in tribunals?

The tribunal which hears your case will normally consist of three people:

The chairperson, who is appointed by the Lord Chancellor; in Scotland, by the Lord President of the Court of Session. They must be barristers or solicitors of at least seven years' experience. There are 65 full-time chairpersons in England and Wales, and 120 part-time chairpersons who also continue their legal practice. In Scotland there are 10 full-time and 16 part-time chairpersons and in the Six Counties 2 full-time and 5 part-time chairpersons.

In each region, those senior chairpersons who take on supervisory duties are known as regional chairpersons. The senior chairperson who exercises supervision over all the tribunals is the president.

The Lord Chancellor has appointed Mr Jack Rumbold to be president of Industrial Tribunals for England and Wales. Mr Rumbold has been a tribunal chairman since 1968 and a regional chairman (London and South) for the past two years.

After war service in the Navy he got a Rhodes Scholarship from New Zealand to Brasenose College, Oxford, where he won a 'blue' at cricket. He was called to the Bar (Inner Temple) in 1948 and became a QC in 1963. It is said that his talk on the work of tribunals at the Annual Institute of Personnel Management Conference in Harrogate last month gave much enlightening pleasure to the many who went to hear him (IDS, *Brief 168*, November 1979).

Full-time chairpersons are appointed until retirement at the age of 72. Part-time chairpersons are appointed for three years at a time. Full-time chairpersons are currently paid £24,000 a year, and part-timers £120 a day. After appointment they are expected to make a detailed study of employment legislation and sit in on hearings before taking cases themselves. They are kept fully up to date with Law Reports and other relevant literature and attend regular briefing conferences.

Two lay members. These are appointed by the Secretary of State for Employment from an employer and an employee panel respectively. Members are appointed for three years at a time. The members of these two panels are selected after consultation between the Department of Employment and the TUC on the one hand (the Scottish TUC is also consulted for Scotland) and the CBI, the Retail Consortium, the Local Authorities' Conditions of Service Advisory Board (and Scottish equivalent) and the Department of Health and Social Security on the other.

In the Six Counties, the Minister of Health and Social Security, the CBI, the Institute of Directors, the Chamber of Commerce and the Irish Congress of Trade Unions are consulted.

To take the basic system: the CBI asks for nominations from amongst its affiliates to regional offices. These nominations should be sponsored and they are looking for those active in, or with past experience of, industrial relations. Suitable nominees are passed on to the Department of Employment. TUC affiliates use different methods. Some unions simply nominate executive members and full-time officials; others allow regional or divisional councils to make nominations from amongst senior officers and lay members. Nominations are also made through the Trade Council machinery. In 1981 the DE ended the TUC monopoly and asked the Managerial, Professional and Staff Liaison Group, a non-union consortium, to make nominations.

There are 2,000 lay members in England and Wales; 225 in Scotland and around 50 in the Six Counties. Approximately 46 per cent of the nominations have been made by the TUC and the same proportion by the CBI. Chairpersons and lay members are allocated to particular cases by the president or regional chairperson. This is generally done by rotation and no attempt is made to place members on the basis of expertise or knowledge of the particular industry or kind of case. An exception is made in cases involving race or sex discrimination and equal pay.

Only eleven chairpersons and under 20 per cent of lay members are women although, for example, about 25 per cent of unfair dismissal cases are brought by women. As far as the legal system is concerned, the union member is not there to represent the union, to act in its interest, or be answerable to fellow members. Union members are there only to contribute experience, and, perhaps the more cynical may say, to legitimise the tribunal.

On appointment, members receive three days training and sit in on hearings. They receive regular copies of the Incomes Data Services *Legal Brief*, and attend two half-day seminars a year to discuss legal developments.

In a normal case, you will be faced by a lawyer, a trade unionist and an employer representative. In certain cases the chairperson can hear the case alone. An example is 'interim relief' (see page 57). In other cases a tribunal member may be asked to sit and it may be discovered that he or she has a connection with the case. In an emergency and with agreement the other two members can hear the case.

Each of the three tribunal members has an equal vote. Sometimes there is disagreement and this leads to what is called a majority decision. Normally this involves one lay member standing out against the chairperson and the other lay member. **In only 4 per cent of cases are 2:1 decisions reached. In only 1 per cent of cases is the chairperson outvoted.**

Union members have up to now played little part in deciding whom the union should nominate and what kind of job they are doing or should be doing. If unions are to continue to support the tribunal system, this area might repay examination and debate.

The structure of industrial tribunals

Industrial tribunals are separately administered in England and Wales, Scotland and the Six Counties. There are Central Offices of Tribunals in London, Glasgow and Belfast. Each central office organises the appointment of members to the tribunals, receives and administers tribunal cases, allocates them to the regions, and organises and supervises the regional tribunals.

The chief executive at the central office is the President of

Industrial Tribunals. This is now a full-time appointment in all three areas. The president will sit as chairperson in tribunals, but the basic job is to supervise the overall working of the tribunals, their operation and procedure. There are 25 tribunal centres in England and Wales, and five in Scotland. In the Six Counties, there are two tribunals in Greater Belfast and they also sit in 13 other towns. There may be four or five tribunals sitting in each centre on a particular day.

The administration of the tribunal system under the president is carried on by the Secretary of the Tribunals and administrative staff, who are civil servants, seconded from their departments to tribunal service.

Industrial tribunals fall under the general supervision of the Council on Tribunals which scrutinises the overall working of tribunals and changes in their procedure. It hears complaints about the general operation of tribunals and reports its findings.

The Employment Appeal Tribunal (EAT)

The EAT hears appeals from tribunals on a point of law. However, if a worker brings a tribunal case on the grounds that he or she has been unreasonably expelled or refused admission to a union with a closed shop, then an appeal from the tribunal decision can be on grounds of law or fact. About 4 per cent of tribunal cases are appealed to the EAT.

The EAT sits in London and Glasgow. Like a tribunal, it will consist of lawyers and lay members. As it is senior to tribunals and generally dealing with more legal matters, the lawyer this time will be a High Court judge nominated by the Lord Chancellor. This judge will sit with two lay members, one management and one union, appointed on the joint recommendation of the Lord Chancellor and Secretary of State for Employment, from nominations made by the TUC and the CBI. The employers' panel, for example, consists of senior personnel and industrial relations managers, such as Len Corran, Director of Personnel with Phillips Industries, and Douglas Anderson, Group Personnel Co-ordinator of the Pilkington Group on the one hand; and the union panel consists of senior union officials, such as Bill Sirs, General Secretary of the Iron and Steel Trades Confederation, and Enoch Humphries, National President of the Fire Brigades Union. A High Court judge acts as the president of the EAT and the registrar monitors cases and advises as to problems of practice and procedure. As with tribunals, the lay members do *not* sit as advisers or assessors but as full members. They have an equal vote and can outvote the judge. **The decisions of the EAT are legally binding on the tribunals.**

The EAT's first president, Mr Justice Phillips, stated its aim as:

> to prevent each tribunal from being a law unto itself . . . to try to introduce into the decisions of something over 60 tribunals up and down the country something in the nature of a uniform approach.

The courts (see figure 1)

Even though you are taking a case to a specialist body, the ordinary courts are still important. If you or the employer lose a case at the EAT, you can appeal on a point of law (see page 14) to the Court of Appeal (Court of Session – Inner House in Scotland). The loser in the Court of Appeal can then appeal further to the House of Lords if permission is granted by the Court of Appeal or by the Appeals Committee of the House of Lords. Appeals will be allowed to the House of Lords where there is a matter of considerable legal importance at stake. You can see this procedure in the diagram on page 11.

Although you can take a case all the way from an industrial tribunal to the House of Lords, this is not likely to happen because the costs are enormous. The National Graphical Association's costs in a recent case involving blacking were £90,000. The amounts usually claimed in compensation will be a tiny proportion of the costs in such cases.

- Since taking a case to the Court of Appeal or the House of Lords can involve a great deal of expense and time and inconvenience, **it is normally only where there is a legal point which can affect a lot of members in future that a union will consider taking the case to the higher court.**
- Similarly, an **employer** will consider appealing a case where he or she thinks that it is not just a matter of Joan Smith who has been dismissed and wants £2,000 compensation, but of a possible 500 *more* Joan Smiths in the near future.
- **Public bodies**, such as the Equal Opportunities Commission and the Commission for Racial Equality, are empowered to finance and take up cases under anti-discrimination

legislation. They may take a case to the higher courts where they feel it to be an issue of public importance which will affect the future development of the legislation.
- **Individuals** can get legal aid for appeals.

The majority of tribunal cases end at tribunals. The majority of cases which are appealed finish at the EAT. A small number of cases go to the higher courts. These cases are, however, legally important because they set precedents which bind the EAT and the industrial tribunals.

The judges in the High Court, the Court of Appeal and the House of Lords are chosen from the ranks of barristers. They will normally be appointed to the High Court then promoted upwards (see Figure 1).

The Court of Appeal sits in two divisions, civil and criminal. Only the first will be important for tribunals.

The House of Lords is the final Appeal Court in the British system.

Precedent

The English legal system is known as an 'adversarial' system. The case is a combat between two sides: (a) to convince the court as to what exactly did happen; and (b) to convince the court as to what law should apply to these facts with each side justifying their argument by reference to past cases or precedents.

A central problem in the system of precedent is this: **When are the facts in past cases the same as in the present case?**

■ In the famous case of *Donoghue v Stevenson* a woman was pouring ginger beer from an opaque bottle when the decomposed remnants of a snail flowed from the bottle. She drank a little, became ill and sued the manufacturers of the drink. The case went all the way to the House of Lords. They decided that a manufacturer in these circumstances was responsible to the consumer if his carelessness caused her harm. Take an imaginary example of a case coming before the courts soon afterwards. A man has discovered a live baby alligator squirming at the bottom of his pint of draught lager. He suffers severe shock and decides to sue the landlord and the brewery. His lawyers might argue that *Donoghue v Stevenson* should be taken as a precedent. The landlord's lawyers could put a whole range of counter arguments – that the precedent only applied

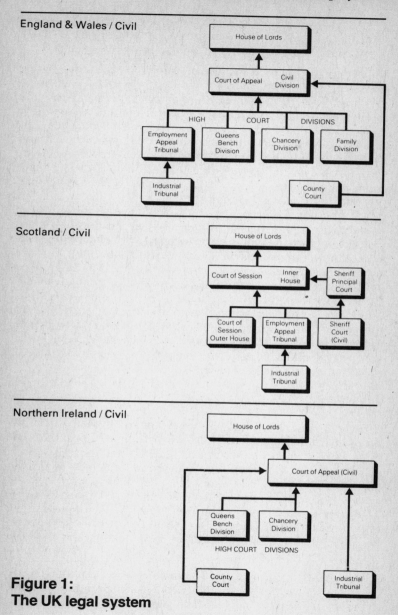

Figure 1:
The UK legal system

to snails not alligators, dead organisms not living ones, soft drinks not beer, that the alligator could have got into the glass by a variety of methods, the snail only at source, and so on.

This is an exaggerated example but it shows the way the law operates.

It was only after this kind of argument had taken place in a number of other cases where the facts differed only slightly, that it became accepted that the precedent set in *Donoghue v Stevenson* was that a manufacturer who sells products in such a fashion that they are likely to reach the ultimate consumer in the form they left the manufacturer with no possibility of intermediate examination owes a duty to the ultimate consumer to take reasonable care to prevent injury.

So, whether a precedent governs another case is not by any means a clear cut matter. **A court has to decide what is the principle in the case that must be followed, the principle that was *vital* to the previous decision.** The court can consider the principle of the previous case *broad* enough to cover the facts before it or *narrow* enough to exclude them. Alternatively it can find that the facts before it are different from the facts in the previous case. In other words, the court can *distinguish* the case it is hearing from the precedents put before them. Obviously **the system of precedent depends on an effective method of reporting cases**. There are several different series of law reports with full details of important cases (see page 117).

Interpretation of statutes

When parliament began to pass more legislation, there was still a problem for the courts in deciding what particular words in an act meant and how they applied to particular facts. The language of an act has to cover a thousand and one eventualities. Is a car a carriage? What about a motor cycle side-car? Is a workroom at the back of a shop a factory? Is a works canteen part of a factory? Language is often broad and imprecise. Parliament cannot foresee *all* the different kinds of cases that may come up; there may be gaps. Cases which decided on these matters are used as precedents in later cases.

- For example, s.14 of the Factories Act 1961 states, 'Every dangerous part of any machinery other than prime movers and transmission machinery shall be securely fenced . . .'

This typical formulation leaves tremendous leeway to the courts. Over the years they decided that 'machinery' did not include machinery being made in the factory or machinery in the course of installation. Machinery was only 'dangerous' if injury was 'reasonably foreseeable'. Moreover, 'the object of the fence was to keep the worker out, not to keep the machine in' said the judges, with little justification from the wording of the act, so that workers were not protected where injured by something coming from out of the machine or where they were injured by their tools rather than themselves coming into contact with the machine.

Precedent in the English legal system

The legal system in this country is distinctive because **precedent has hardened into a rigid system: the decisions of the higher courts bind lower courts.**

- **Industrial tribunals** are bound by the decisions of the EAT, the Court of Appeal and the House of Lords.
- **The EAT** is bound by the decisions of the Court of Appeal and the House of Lords.
- **The Court of Appeal** is bound by the decisions of the House of Lords. The Court of Appeal (Civil Division) binds itself for the future unless it believes that the previous decision was made in error, there are two conflicting decisions, or they have been corrected by the House of Lords.
- **The House of Lords** will treat former decisions of the House as normally binding but will depart from a decision where they think it right to do so.

One tribunal is *not* bound by the decision of another. However, if you cite the decision of another tribunal as a precedent in your case then the chair should find it *persuasive*, i.e. strongly consider its application. The EAT, the most important body for case law affecting the tribunals, has stated that only decisions giving authoritative rulings on the interpretation of unclear and ambiguous legislation should be regarded as being binding (*Jowett v Earl of Bradford* No. 2 1978 ICR 431).

Remember:
(1) **The higher courts are important**, even though you may never get to them. What happens there influences your tribunal case.

(2) **The higher courts make law.** Although judges would assert that they are simply interpreting the will of Parliament, the final decision is theirs and whatever a tribunal may think it has to follow those decisions. Don't just look at the tribunals. **Look at the system.**

Points of law

Appeals are generally only allowed on a **point of law. A point of law will include:**

- any point of **statutory interpretation**. Have the tribunal misunderstood the meaning of constructive dismissal, failed to grasp the statutory meaning of redundancy or failed to consider the cases interpreting the meaning of 'employee'? If so, they have got the law wrong and an appeal is on;
- questions involving the **general common law**. For example, a tribunal may have implied a term into a Bolton worker's contract that he will work anywhere in Lancashire when, on the general principles of the law of contract, they should not have done so, and he should be employed only at Bolton and is therefore redundant when switched to Saint Helens because the Bolton factory is closed;
- cases where the appeal court decides that the inferior court could not have possibly reached the legal or practical conclusion they did **on the evidence before them**;
- a tribunal which does not follow the **correct procedure** contained in its rules. If it could be shown that with no justification the tribunal refused to allow a party to cross-examine the other side's witnesses, then a point of law would be involved; and
- a tribunal which exercises its discretion on **wrong principles**. If, for example, it unjustifiably refuses to allow an adjournment.

The judges

In the early days of legislation tribunals may have had a lot of discretion in interpreting the law. As time goes on and there are more appeals, tribunals are increasingly administering the law laid down elsewhere by the judges. There are tighter limits on their discretion. For example, the president of the EAT recently commented:

In short, the Appeal Tribunal started by taking a broad view of what was a point of law so as to seek to state and apply principles of fair industrial practice; it is now bound by authority to take a narrower view of what is a point of law and in consequence its role as the arbiter of what is good industrial practice is much reduced. (Mr Justice Browne-Wilkinson, 'The Role of the Employment Appeal Tribunal in the 1980s', *ILJ*, vol. 11, no. 2, June 1982.)

When considering how judges operate, it is worth remembering the words of the present Lord Chancellor, Lord Hailsham: 'there is no such thing as a value-free or neutral interpretation of the law' ('Equality and the Law', *The Listener*, 6 June 1974).

Many trade unionists will be familiar with the statement Lord Justice Scrutton made in 1920:

The habits you are trained in, the people with whom you mix lead to your having a certain class of ideas of such a nature that when you have to deal with other ideas you do not give as sound and accurate judgements as you would wish . . . Labour says 'Where are your impartial judges? They all move in the same circle as the employers and they are all educated and nursed in the same ideas as the employers. How can a labour man or a trade unionist get impartial justice?' It is very difficult sometimes to be sure that you have put yourself in a thoroughly impartial position between two disputants one of your own class and one not of your own class.

The class background from which judges come and the social role they play is important. In his book *The Politics of the Judiciary*,* Professor Griffith examines all the evidence of the background and social class of judges in the higher court over the last century:

Over the whole period the dominance of the upper and middle class is overwhelming . . . four out of five full time professional judges are products of public school and of Oxford or Cambridge.

The same point is made by Professor Miliband in his book, *The State in Capitalist Society*.*

---

*See page 249 for details.

The judicial elites like other elites of the State system are mainly drawn from the upper and middle layers of society, and those judges who are not have clearly come to belong to those layers by the time they reach the bench.

On the whole and particularly in periods of social upheaval, the judges' decisions have applied the law against the interests of trade unionists.

Little has changed since Scrutton spoke in the 1920s. In the 1970s another prominent judge, Lord Devlin, could say:

Judges are inevitably part of the establishment and the establishment's ideas are those which are operating in our minds . . . I think the law has to be part of the establishment. (A. Paterson, *The Law Lords*.)*

Advisory, Conciliation and Arbitration Service (ACAS)

The main work of ACAS is to provide advice, conciliation and arbitration to both sides of industry, when they have industrial relations problems and disputes.

It is given a specific job in relation to industrial tribunals: to offer its conciliation services to mend fences between both sides, with the hope that the dispute can be settled without a tribunal hearing. The argument is that many cases will be amenable to settlement by the parties themselves and ACAS can act as a stimulus and a sieve.

ACAS call this pre-tribunal role individual conciliation. Of course, you, your members or your employer may have been involved with the conciliation officer wearing a general industrial relations hat, when there is only a potential dismissal and before a tribunal application has occurred. Nevertheless, when the application goes in you will see the CO again, this time wearing a tribunal helper hat. About one third of complaints to tribunals are settled by conciliation. However, the median figure agreed for compensation through the conciliation process is *less than £500*. The median figure for awards made by the tribunal after a decision is £963. On the other hand, you have to win first . . .

---

*See page 249 for details.

Regulations

These are secondary legislation made under authority given to the Secretary of State for Employment by legislation. **They are law.** If, for example, the relevant industrial tribunal regulations are not followed in your case, then you can appeal. The procedures of industrial tribunals are governed by the *Industrial Tribunals (Rules of Procedure) Regulations 1980* (SI 884). The procedural regulations in Scotland (SI 885) and the Six Counties (1981 SI 188) are now almost identical. These regulations are wide and state specifically that tribunals should be as informal as possible and, outside the rules specified, regulate their own procedure. It is useful to have a copy of these regulations, which are available from HMSO.

Codes of Practice

Codes of Practice specifically relevant to tribunal cases have been those on *Disciplinary Procedures* and *Time Off*, although the 1972 *Code of Industrial Relations Practice* and the ACAS Code on *Disclosure of Information* have also been relevant. These documents have now been joined by government Codes of Practice on *Picketing* and on the *Closed Shop*. Codes of Practice are intended to go into greater detail than the provisions of the legislation, to give examples to explain points in greater detail or to suggest procedures for making the legislation work. They are guidance to be taken into account by the tribunals but **they are not law**.

The tendency has been for tribunals, under pressure from the higher courts, to pay less attention to Codes of Practice in recent years. However, **you should always look through all the Codes to see if there is anything relevant to your case**.

Representation

The tribunal rules state that either party to a case may represent themselves or be represented by a barrister, a solicitor, a trade union or employers' association representative, or by any other person she or he chooses as representative.

■ In one case a manager conducted the case and was a substantial witness. He had also been a member of the Appeals Board which heard the worker's appeal against his dismissal. 'It can obviously give rise to misunderstanding if a man who has appeared as a member of an Appeal Board subsequently appears at the tribunal . . . as an advocate as it were officially representing the respondent employer. To do so can obviously give rise to misunderstandings however ill founded in the mind of the employee. We think that as far as possible such a course should be avoided.' (*Singh v London Country Bus Services Ltd* (1976) IRLR 176, EAT).

There has been a big increase in the number of lawyers handling cases in tribunals. In 1980, about 35 per cent of all workers and about 51 per cent of employers had legal representation. Workers were represented by union representatives in a further 16 per cent of cases.

- Some unions have officers who specialise in taking cases to tribunals.
- In other situations, somebody from the union legal department may handle a case where it is felt that some legal point is involved.
- In some cases, convenors or stewards argue cases after consultation with the full-time officer. The Code of Practice, *Time off for Trade Union Duties*, specifically allows paid time off for this.

In most cases, however, where the union is involved a full-time official will argue the case before the tribunal.

We have pointed out that, while many cases turn on the facts and broad principles, the legal points are becoming more and more important. It is not beyond any full-time officer to master these legal points. The problem is one of time. If the present tendency towards legalism continues, then unions will need to consider specialist appointments of tribunal officers.

At the moment too much is put on the shoulders of officers in the field who sometimes receive minimal back up from legal and research services.

The situation is more difficult when you are taking an appeal to the EAT. The EAT thinks that non-lawyers may not be the best representatives. One full-time official who represented a member was informed,

it is unfortunate that the respondent should not have had the benefit of legal representation in a case of such importance . . . unions who adopt this policy before the Appeal Tribunal in cases which involve important principles of law do a disservice rather than a service to their members. *(Edward Gardiner & Sons Ltd v Cassidy* (1977) EAT 826/77.)

On the other hand, NUJ National Organiser, Linda Rogers, recently became the first union official to take on and beat a barrister retained by the employer in an EAT case involving the dismissal of an NUJ member by UCATT (*The Journalist*, August 1980).

Legal Aid

Legal aid is not available for representation in industrial tribunal cases. The TUC has opposed its extension on the grounds that more lawyers would lead to more legalism. Instead it has argued that government money should be made available to existing bodies which provide lay representation but which might call on lawyers for difficult cases. The Royal Commission on Legal Services has recommended that **legal aid should be available for appearances before tribunals**:

- where a significant point of law arises;
- where the evidence is complex or specialised;
- where a test case arises; or
- where the ability of a worker to follow an occupation is at stake.

Legal aid is available for advice, help with filling in an IT 1 (see page 70), writing to the employer, and so on. If your income and savings are within certain laid down limits then you have the right to advice from a solicitor up to the value of £40, free or at a reduced rate. Your means are assessed by reference to your disposable income – what you have left from your net pay minus allowances for dependants and such matters as rent. The unemployed will generally be covered.

You apply for legal help by filling in the Law Society's Green Form. You have to make sure that any solicitor you get in touch with is in the Legal Advice Scheme and also that they have some knowledge of labour law matters and tribunal cases. While the solicitors cannot argue your case before the tribunal under this scheme, they can do most of the preparatory work up to the hearing. You should use the solicitor to: get general advice; to help in filling in your application form; to assist you in preparing evidence and writing letters; to give you some help in preparing your presentation for the tribunal. If the case is a difficult one the £40 limit can be extended so that, for example, the solicitor can get a barrister's opinion on complex problems. If you do not qualify for the legal advice scheme you should ask a solicitor for a fixed fee interview. Most will give you half an hour's advice for around £5.

Another possibility for those without the support of a union is to get in touch with one of the Law Centres which exist in most big cities. They will give free advice and may be willing to represent you. Citizens Advice Bureaux are basically useful for putting you in touch with people who can give you the help you need. ACAS also has a general obligation to give you advice, though it will not take up a case for you. If you have problems involving discrimination at work, the first thing you should do is get in touch with the Equal Opportunities Commission or the Commission for Racial Equality. They will give you advice, legal assistance and sometimes legal representation – where the case is complex or raises an issue of principle.

From an applicant's point of view, however, this situation is unsatisfactory. It shows that trade-union membership which offers specialist advice is a good investment against times of trouble when you may need the law. (See page 244 for useful addresses.)

Let us now try to sum up some of the good points and bad points of industrial tribunals.

Advantages of tribunals

Lay members

The ordinary courts have often arrived at decisions harmful to workers not simply because of bias, but because of their ignorance of what goes on in industry, or failure to grasp the significance of certain practices.

The idea of involving lay members is to some degree to constitute an 'industrial jury' and to provide people who will understand the intricacies of a payment by results system, the significance of a 'status quo' clause, how a particular piece of machinery operates, as well as the practical problems and different attitudes which occur at work.

Speed of hearing

Workers want a quick hearing and a quick remedy when they are involved with the law. They may be out of work, injured or sick, and without resources to fall back on. Taking a Health and Safety claim to the High Court can take two years. If one side is to appeal further, a case could take three or four years. **Tribunals work much quicker.** The most recent figures show a time lag of 13 weeks. It can take from nine weeks to nine months from application to hearing according to when you apply, the complexity of your case, how serious conciliation is and whether you use mechanisms such as a request for further particulars (see page 133). Fortunes can vary.

■ Two men were sacked for allegedly committing identical clocking offences on 1 March 1978. A's case was heard on 27 April. It was completed in a day. He was represented by his union. B applied to the tribunal later than A. There were problems of procedure and he was not represented. The case lasted all day 12 June and all day 24 July. Neither side knew the result until 13 October 1978.

Eighty per cent of tribunal hearings are completed within one day and 95 per cent in two days.

Cost

The cost of a tribunal hearing is likely to be less than that of a case taken to the ordinary courts. On the other hand, the fact that there is no legal aid can make life difficult for the unrepresented applicant.

Informality

In comparison with the courts, the tribunal proceedings are informal. They try as much as possible to avoid the technicalities of procedure. On the other hand, don't expect a double brandy and a cigar and a hearty 'tell me all about it old son'. There is a basic procedure which must be followed.

Whilst the tribunals attempt to keep the hearing simple and sometimes object to lawyers introducing legal technicalities and pyrotechnics, it is not possible to stop lawyers using legal methods, and legal representation is increasing (see page 26). There may in future be a greater tendency to legalism and discussion of precedents in tribunals because of the legal background of chairpersons, increased legal representation, the use of legal concepts in legislation and the system of appeals.

■ In the Court of Appeal dealing with the growing complexities of the Equal Pay Act, Lord Justice Lawton commented that industrial tribunals were originally intended to be flexible and informal bodies. 'If the wording of the relevant statutes has opened the door to legal subtleties there is nothing the courts can do to stop what I regard as an unfortunate development. The remedy lies with parliament . . . the courts should lean in favour of simplicity of meaning which will safeguard informality of procedure' (*Clay Cross (Quarry Service) Ltd v Fletcher* (1979) 1 AER 474 CA). Lord Denning has also pointed out: 'If we are not careful we shall find industrial tribunals bent down under the weight of law books or, what is worse, asleep under them' (*Walls Meat Co. v Khan* (1978) IRLR 499 CA). An academic lawyer reviewing recent developments feels, 'The prospects are that tribunals will come to behave increasingly like courts simply because there is nothing sufficiently fundamental to differentiate them from courts' (R. Munday, 'Tribunal Lore', *ILJ* vol. 10, no. 3, September 1981).

So the advantages of industrial tribunals are limited and may be more so in the future. Nevertheless, you may be in a situation where you have no alternative. Tribunals may help the poorly organised, particularly blacks or women workers in particular circumstances when they have nothing left to rely on.

■ **How did you get the sack?** 'Last spring management announced redundancies. They'd got rid of the odd part-timer before without any challenge from the union – we're all in the T&G, though it isn't a closed shop – so they tried to give 60 of the 75 part-timers who work here the push straight away. By the way, all the part-timers are women, and some of them had been here 17 years.'

What did the union do? 'Well, you've got to remember that it took us women years even to get two representatives on the shop stewards' committee. A long time ago I used to be pretty active in the union, but when I tried to stand as a shop steward I was told I couldn't because I was part-time. When my dismissal came up it was the same story. The management asked for a formal agreement with the union that part-timers should be the first to go, and the convenor, Alan Care, went along with it. It was put to a mass meeting, and of course, being in a minority, us part-timers didn't have a chance. After the meeting a lot of men thought better of it because of the length of time many of the women had worked here. But the convenor stood up for the firm. When I went to him about it he said there was nothing he could do.'

So what did you do? 'I couldn't accept it. If I'd just gone out of the gate feeling upset nothing would have happened. I was sure we had a case, so I wrote to the National Council for Civil Liberties in London for Anne Sedley's pamphlet on part-time workers. I read it, found that I had a case as I suspected, and phoned her up. She said I was right and went to the Equal Opportunities Commission who said they'd be prepared to pay my costs.'

What happened next? 'This time last year 20 of us went to a tribunal. Sandra Powell won because she couldn't go full-time, but the rest of us lost because our kids were grown up and we were technically available for full-time work – even though we didn't want it. So we appealed. Eventually, it got down to 14 of us. Some of us had been out of work for 12 months and five had husbands who were out of work too. Things got so desperate that, to avoid losing my case, I took Eley up on an offer of temporary employment they gave me, even though I'm on a monthly contract and don't like the work (it's heavy and dangerous, because it involves loading powder into bullets).'

What was the result of the appeal? 'We won. The judge ruled that it was unfair dismissal and gross sex discrimination – too right! It was a great victory, not only for me and 13 others, but for women everywhere. They'll have to pay us back wages too. But they can still appeal against the ruling, so we're on our guard.' (From *The Next Step*, November 1982.)

Disadvantages of industrial tribunals

Poor results

If we take unfair dismissal we find:

- there has been a marked downward trend in the number of decisions favourable to workers from 1975 to 1981. In 1975, workers won in two out of five cases before a tribunal (39.6

per cent). In 1981, workers had only a one in four chance of winning an unfair dismissal case (23.3 per cent actually won). Even these figures do not tell the whole story, given the amount of cases withdrawn, settled for a small sum or dismissed;

● reinstatement or re-engagement was the remedy in 93 and 57 cases respectively out of 13,436 cases heard at industrial tribunals in 1981. In 0.8 per cent of cases the applicant was actually taken back. In other words, if you get a tribunal hearing, you have less than a one in 10,000 chance of getting the job back. The use of reinstatement and re-engagement at the conciliation stage was also limited, representing together 1.8 per cent of all cases settled at the conciliation stage;

● the median award for compensation in dismissal cases in 1978 was £375, in 1979 £401, and in 1981 £963. In 1981 more than half the awards were for amounts less than £1,000;

● in equal pay and sex discrimination cases in 1982, under 20 per cent of the decisions were in favour of the applicants. This compares with a 30 per cent success rate in 1976. If your case is heard under the Race Relations Act, you have only a one in 20 chance of winning.

Even if you win – and that is not easy – you generally end up with peanuts.

Limitations of laws

Under present legislation:

● employers cannot be compelled to reinstate a worker, no matter how disgraceful their conduct;

● employers cannot be stopped from making workers redundant, no matter how trivial their economic or social justification;

● a tribunal cannot order an employer to allow a steward a certain amount of time off. They can only order an employer to pay a steward who has taken time off for that past occurrence.

Many of the laws show how little progress workers have made in this area in the 1980s:

● workers can go on strike but if the employer sacks all of them without exception then they have no legal rights;

- workers are not even allowed basic free speech by being entitled to picket workplaces other than their own;
- the law provides no guarantee of the basic right to union recognition.

Our laws on unfair dismissal and maternity are among the worst in the EEC. This is because in introducing the employment laws that tribunals deal with, parliament did not start from the needs of workers or the need to strengthen the trade-union movement. This is so even where laws *appear* to be favourable to workers.

In introducing the Redundancy Payments Bill into parliament in 1965, Ray Gunter, the then minister, said:

> One of our most urgent needs is to use our manpower more effectively. We have far too many restrictive practices, too much overmanning . . . (the Bill) has an important and necessary part to play in allaying fears of redundancy and resistance to new methods and economic change . . . our object is to increase mobility of labour by reducing resistance to change.

Professor Grunfeld in his book, *The Law of Redundancy*, speaks of:

> the paramount policy of the Act . . . to enable British management . . . to achieve needed economies in the use of labour . . . and the *subsidiary effect* of the drafting of the Act to provide certain employees in certain limited circimstances with compensation (emphasis added).

When introducing unfair dismissal provisions the politicians are not primarily concerned with the man or woman on the cobbles. Albert Booth remarked on the Employment Protection Bill:

> The government are particularly concerned about cases in which employees are dismissed for trade union membership or activity especially because such dismissals are more likely to give rise to industrial disputes than most other reasons for dismissal (*Hansard*, 28 April 1975).

The Incomes Data Service has noted:

> Speaking to the National Chamber of Trade this month the Employment Secretary asked, 'how much more certain was the wild cat strike before the tribunal remedy was introduced?' Mr Booth's question was rhetorical. He believes that

strikes over dismissals have been much reduced and that costs in terms of 'money, time and effort' of any strike over a dismissal far outweighs the cost of being the respondent in a tribunal application (IDS, *Brief 121*, November 1977).

The real reason most of the last Labour government's employment legislation was passed was to enable management to run their business more efficiently. The idea was to change workers' behaviour so that, when they had a problem whether over a sacking, time off for a steward or equal pay, they would not use the most efficient method of getting a result: direct negotiation backed by the ability to take industrial action. Instead they would take the matter into a legal procedure which is less effective. Take unfair dismissal. If a steward is victimised and you take strike action then you have a fighting chance of getting the job back. If you take the case to a tribunal you have little chance.

A tribunal case is no substitute for building up that bargaining power. If unions get used to taking cases to tribunals rather than using union strength, industrial muscle will become flabby through lack of use.

Judges' attitudes

In a capitalist society the law may limit the rights of capital. It will not control capital's mainsprings, the ownership and control of the means of production. **The law limits the rights of capital in order ultimately to protect capitalist property.** This ethic is un-reservedly accepted by the judiciary as a social body. They ensure that the limitations do not go too far.

We cannot talk about tribunals in isolation from the legal system. They are part of that system and in the end answerable to it. Look at some of the attitudes in the Employment Appeal Tribunal.

- **unconscious racism:** in one case an Asian worker, suddenly faced at a tribunal hearing with reasons for his sacking which had never been given before, asked for an adjourn-ment to consider them. The EAT judge, Kilner Brown, expressed his impatience with this very reasonable be-haviour and said, 'This is somewhat typical of the oriental mind if one may say so without disrespect.' *Rajguru v Top Order* (1978) ICR 565.

- **political bias:** judges are not supposed to indulge in politics yet Mr Justice Phillips, the first President of the EAT, could state,

  > It can scarcely be thought to be straying into the field of politics to observe that the system of labour law is remarkedly lopsided. Thus there is a complete withdrawal of the law from the field of industrial disputes and trade unions in many respects remain outside the law (*Industrial Law Journal* vol. 7, 1978, p. 237).

- **blatant sexism:** as you go up the ladder the reactionary social attitudes become clearer. As Lord Denning said in an important case dealing with the Sex Discrimination Act:

  > I must say that it would be very wrong to my mind if this statute were thought to obliterate the differences between men and women or to do away with the chivalry and courtesy which we expect mankind to give womankind. The natural differences of sex must be regarded even in the interpretation of an Act of Parliament (*Automotive Products Ltd v F. W. Peake* (1977) IRLR 365 CA).

With attitudes like this, it is not surprising that the courts get it right for the bosses and wrong for women, blacks, and all trade unionists. Nor are the tribunals immune. As early as 1975, one study found that tribunals had adopted 'an essentially managerial perspective' and in developing the law had failed to

> examine critically the commercial judgement of employers in, say, declaring a redundancy situation or adversely assessing the ability of an individual to meet managerial expectations of his job. Still less did they challenge the right of employers to make such a judgement (*Industrial Relations and the Limits of Law* – see back of book for details).

This is still the case. Phillips in the EAT said, 'It is important that the operation of the legislation should not impede employers unreasonably in the efficient management of their business which must be in the interests of all.' One legal commentator feels that,

> the law of unfair dismissal has been sterilised to such an extent that it is reasonable to conclude that far from controlling

managerial discretion and therefore protecting the interests of workers in job security, the law generally endorses and legitimates a strong conception of managerial authority. (H. Collins, 'Capitalist Discipline and Corporatist Law', *ILJ* vol. 11, no. 3, September 1982).

So if you are considering taking a case to an industrial tribunal then you need to be absolutely clear in your own mind as to . . .

What tribunals are and what they are not

Industrial tribunals are basically similar to National Insurance and Supplementary Benefit Appeals Tribunals. If you are faced with a situation where management wishes to declare redundancies, you do not normally think of packing your briefcase for a social security tribunal hearing. You roll up your sleeves to fight the redundancy. If you do end up before a social security tribunal you realise that you have lost the main battle. All you are fighting for now is welfare benefit.

The same is true about industrial tribunals. **All you are fighting for in most tribunal cases is unemployment benefit, not the dismissal of a worker. Cash compensation is no substitute for a job. And neither is the industrial tribunal a substitute for trade union action.**

The idea that industrial tribunals can help unions influence or challenge basic management decisions is a con trick. Industrial tribunals can only minimise, or help a worker deal with, the consequences of those decisions.

Before you consider taking a case to a tribunal, always be sure that all other methods have failed. You should consider:

- how important the problem is to the member, the workplace organisation, other members. How important the issue really is to the employer;
- if it is an important issue, have you exhausted all possibilities of achieving a desirable solution through negotiation? Can you, for example, involve any other levels of management and/or the union?
- if you have exhausted all peaceful means, have you considered industrial action? Have you analysed and discussed with other union officials, the relevant stewards and members, the market position of the employer, the overall

economic position and the potential losses to the employer and workers? Crucially, have you thought about the members' attitudes and the difference aggressive tactics, such as picketing and occupations, may make?

- are you sure the basic facts of the case and the issues involved have been made clear to the membership? If you feel that strike action is necessary, have you exhausted all methods of convincing the membership that it is essential?

- if you feel that neither further negotiation nor industrial action is on, then you need to consider other factors – such as qualifications, time limits and costs – before deciding that a tribunal hearing is your best bet (see pages 30, 48, 200).

3.

Are you qualified?

Table 1 (page 44) gives you some basic information on whether you qualify to take a case to a tribunal. It is important that you look at this when deciding whether you have a case. In the second column of the table, you will see the time limits you must keep to if your case is to be heard. There are exceptions to these and they are dealt with in greater detail in the next chapter. **What you need to do now is:**

- Confirm that your problem is in the list of **workers' rights** which tribunals deal with, in the first column of Table 1. If you want to know more about what is involved in these rights and exactly what kind of situations they cover, look at two other books in this series, *Rights at Work* and *Employment Law Under the Tories* by Jeremy McMullen (Pluto).
- If you decide that what has happened to you could be in breach of one of the legal rights listed, then see whether you are one of the workers covered by this right. These rights cover only **employees**. You must first establish that you *are* an employee so have a look at the explanation of this on page 31.
- Even if you are an employee, you are not yet home and dry. Check through the fourth column in the table to establish that you are not one of the groups of employees specifically **excluded from certain legal rights**. On page 33 and page 34 we look at two of the particular problems associated with these exclusions, employees working abroad and normal retirement age.
- Check that you are not an employee who is on a **fixed term contract** and who has given up his or her legal rights, page 35.
- Look at the third column in the table to ensure that you have the required **continuous service** to qualify to take up a

a tribunal case involving a particular right. The way the lawyers calculate continuous employment is explained on page 37. The rules for calculating continuous employment are contained in the EP(C)A Schedule 13.

Who is an employee?

An employee is somebody who is employed under a contract of employment. Disputes often occur in courts or tribunals as to whether a worker is employed under a contract of employment or is self-employed working under a contract for services.

Courts have used different tests to see whether a worker is an employee or self-employed. These are:

- **control:** at first the courts said you were an employee if your boss had the right to control the way in which you worked, the right to tell you how, when and where to do your job. It soon became obvious that this did not help with skilled craftworkers who were employed under a contract of employment but could not be controlled in this sense, still less a surgeon in the operating theatre;

- **organisation:** the courts next asked whether the worker's job was an integral part of the business or only an accessory to it. Lord Denning compared a ship's captain, a chauffeur and a newspaper reporter with a ship's pilot, a taxi driver and a freelance journalist. The first three had a contract of employment, the second three did not. Other judges said the basic question was: was the work done for the organisation or was the person in business on his or her own account?

- **mixed test:**
  - In one case drivers were described in writing as self-employed. The company arranged for them to buy their own lorries on hire purchase terms paid for from their enhanced earnings. They were paid by the mile, subject to a guaranteed minimum. How and when they worked was for them to decide and they could even delegate the driving. They were required to paint the lorry in the company's name, have it maintained at the company's garages and obey company instructions when on the premises. The court said that the test was a 'mixed' one. You had to look at a number of factors, none of which is conclusive, including control and organisation, and also

wages, pensions, and the social security position. Also important was the intention of the parties although this was not conclusive (*Ready Mixed Concrete Ltd v Minister of Pensions* (1968) 2QB 497 HC).

This last is the test generally used today. It gives tribunals and courts a great deal of discretion and illustrates that after 100 years they have not really succeeded in laying down clear rules, they are simply saying we will use our idea of common sense to see if this particular relationship looks like a contract of employment.

Here is an example of how tribunals deal with this problem:

■ Mrs Cope worked at home assembling shoes. She was given training, told how to do the work and supplied with patterns and materials. She was paid wages each week without deduction of tax or national insurance, received no holiday or sick pay and was paid only for work which the company found acceptable. The EAT upheld the tribunal decision that Mrs Cope was an employee, not in business on her own account. She implicitly accepted the company's control and was in reality an employee working in her own home as a matter of convenience (*Airfix Footwear Ltd v Cope* (1978) IRLR 396 EAT).

Similarly, tribunals have decided that casual workers are employees when they have agreed to work certain hours suitable to them and have *no option* but to turn up to work those hours when work is offered; but they are not employees when they are merely *invited* to work from time to time and have the *choice* of accepting the offer or not (*Mailway Southern Ltd v Willsher* (1978) IRLR 322 EAT; *Miller v Harry Thornton (Lollies) Ltd* (1978) IRLR 430).

Another practice which has caused problems has been the Lump — labour-only sub-contracting in the building industry. Here, workers who agree with a sub-contractor that the sub-contractor will find them work with a main contractor are generally self-employed and not employees.

However, even here the line between employee and independent contractor is a thin one.

■ The Court of Appeal decided that, for example, where a worker was hired on a labour-only sub-contracting basis with the intention that he was self-employed he was *in fact* an employee. Despite their intention, the realities of the situation were that he was provided with tools, told by the foreman how to work, when to move from site to site and paid wages on an hourly basis: in reality he was an employee (*Ferguson v Dawson & Partners* (1976) IRLR 346 CA).

The complications of this type of arrangement have even led the courts to say that there are other types of relationship besides employer/employee and self-employed/client.

■ Labour Force Ltd supplied workers to building firms. They took on workers on a sub-contract basis and supplied them to contractors to work on sites. The workers were paid by Labour Force Ltd but their work was directed by the contractors. The High Court upheld a tribunal decision that the workers were self-employed but felt that this kind of situation where A contracts with B to work for C was 'a different kind of contract from either of the familiar two' (*Construction Industry Training Board v Labour Force Ltd* (1970) 5 ITR 290 HC).

Where there is an agreement between the employer and the worker that the worker should be regarded as self-employed she or he may still, as far as the law is concerned, be an employee and entitled to an employee's legal rights. The parties cannot alter the reality of a relationship.

■ Where there was evidence that a bar steward was labelled self-employed, the EAT applied this test and found he was in reality an employee. 'If you had asked him while he was working 'are you your own boss?' could he honestly have given any answer other than 'no'? (*Withers v Flackwell Heath FC Supporters Club* (1981) IRLR 307 EAT).

Employees working abroad

Tribunals and courts have found it difficult to decide whether only workers who 'ordinarily work in Great Britain' can bring a tribunal case. For example, a staff consultant worked abroad for substantial periods of time. The EAT held that he could not claim unfair dismissal before an industrial tribunal. What proportion of working time he spent abroad and at home was not important. The question was: did he work abroad in the ordinary performance of his contract *as well as* in the UK? If he did, he could not claim.

This decision was overruled by the Court of Appeal. A person cannot *at the same time* be said to be ordinarily working both inside and outside the UK. To decide the question you should not simply look at the proportions of time actually spent inside our outside the UK. **You should look at all the terms, express and implied, of the contract of employment.** The test is where the employer's *base* is, the place where the employee is to be treated as ordinarily working. **The terms which show you the employer's base include:**

- where the headquarters are;
- where the travels involved in the job begin and end;
- where the home is or is expected to be;
- where and in what currency she or he is paid;
- does he or she pay National Insurance contributions in the UK? (*Wilson v Maynard Shipbuilding Consultants AB* (1977) IRLR 491 CA.)

On this basis an airlines pilot who spent most of his time outside Great Britain was held to ordinarily work here (*Todd v British Midland Airways Ltd* (1978) IRLR 370 CA.)

An exception to this general rule is that a worker who is in this country at the date of dismissal in accordance with instructions is entitled to a redundancy payment but not unfair dismissal (*Costain Civil Engineering Ltd v Draycott* (1977) IRLR 17 EAT).

Normal retirement age

If there is a normal retirement age for a particular job then you will be **disqualified from claiming certain rights** once you reach that age whether it is above or below state pension age.

- If – and only if – there is no normal retiring age for your job, you will be disqualified from claiming certain rights once you reach the age of 60 (women) and 65 (men).
- The normal retiring age is the age at which the workers involved are required to retire unless their employment is extended by mutual agreement.

   ■ Mrs Notham was sacked from her job as a teacher when she was 61. Her conditions of employment said, 'the employment of a teacher will terminate automatically at the end of the term during which he reached his 65th birthday.' Mrs Notham was not excluded from bringing a claim for unfair dismissal. There was a normal retiring age and it was 65. The fact that 60 was the pensionable age for women was neither here nor there (*Notham v London Borough of Barnet* (1979) IRLR 35 HL).

Following this case the Court of Appeal have said that the normal retiring age is to be found by looking at your contract. If that specifies an age at which you can be compulsorily retired, that is the normal retiring age – even though you may be retained after that age by agreement with the employer (*Howard v Dept National Savings Ltd* (1981) IRLR 40 CA). In this case the court disapproved of another Court of Appeal decision (*The Post Office v Wallser* (1981) IRLR 37 CA), in which it had been stated that normal retiring age does not depend on your contract but is a question of all the evidence, for example, what is the position for other workers in your category or grade?

The EAT in a case involving Mrs Duke, a clerk, said that the relevant question was 'what is the retiring age for clerks in the company?' not the contractual position of Mrs Duke as an individual (*Duke v Reliance Systems* (1982) IRLR 347 EAT). So the law here is a little confused.

Fixed term contracts

If you are on a fixed term contract and it expires, then you are taken to be dismissed and can claim some of your legal rights. **There are, however, a number of exceptions:**

- if you have a fixed term contract for **two years or more**, and if you specifically agreed in writing before it expired that you would not claim when the contract expired, you are excluded from claiming a redundancy payment;
- if a fixed term contract for **one year or more** was made after 1 October 1980, and you agree to give up your rights in writing before the contract expired, then you cannot claim unfair dismissal. The exclusion clause only operates when you are dismissed because the contract ends. If you are sacked before this date you can take a case to a tribunal;
- a fixed term contract may include a clause saying it can be **ended by notice**. Contracts for limited periods on building sites or involving research or teaching staff in universities

or colleges which normally contain notice periods can therefore be fixed term contracts within the legislation.

■ Mr Dixon and Mr Constanti were employed as porters by the BBC under 'a temporary engagement for an indefinite period', a series of fixed term contracts which included a term that the contract could be terminated at a week's notice. The Court of Appeal held that, despite the notice terms, the contracts were still fixed term contracts (*BBC v Dixon, BBC v Constanti* (1979) IRLR 114 CA);

● if the original fixed term contract which contains an exclusion clause **is renewed**, the original exclusion clause will not govern the extra period.

■ X is a Research Officer at Grantchester Polytechnic on a two year contract which contains an exclusion clause. At the end of the period his project gets funds for another year. The original exclusion clause will not govern the renewal of X's job for the further 12 months. This is a separate fixed term contract. There must be a separate exclusion for unfair dismissal after 1 October 1980 and there can be no exclusion for the purpose of redundancy payments as the contract is for less than two years (*BBC v Ioannou* (1975) IRLR 184 CA; *Open University v Triesman* (1978) IRLR 114 EAT).

For a contract to be classified as a fixed term contract it must be a contract with a defined beginning and a defined end. A contract to achieve a certain task or performance with no specific finishing date is *not* a fixed term contract.

■ Mrs Guy worked as a part-time teacher at Swindon College. She was paid by the hour and at the start of each academic year entered a fresh contract of employment under which it was agreed that she would work on specified days of the week. She stopped work each academic year whenever the courses she was involved with were finished, so she did not work right up to the end of the academic year. When her appointment was not renewed, she claimed unfair dismissal but her employers argued that as there was no fixed term contract there had been no dismissal. The Court of Appeal agreed that this was not a fixed term contract but a contract which is discharged by performance. When this kind of contract is fulfilled there is no dismissal (*Wiltshire County Council v NATFHE and Guy* (1980) IRLR 198 CA).

Continuous employment

The rules governing this are contained in the EP(C)A sch. 13. Most of the legislation presumes that your employment *is* continuous. Your boss has to prove that it is not (*Nicoll v Nocorrode Ltd* (1981) IRLR 163 EAT). One exception is the right to written particulars and statutory notice periods. Your position as regards continuity should be stated in your written particulars of terms and conditions of employment. Only those weeks count towards continuity during which your contract requires you to work a certain number of hours, *whether or not* you are at work that week, or you *actually* work those hours. **The basic figure is 16 hours**. Each week counts in which you are employed under a contract to work 16 hours or more a week.

Contract for 16 hours or more a week

If you work under a contract to work 16 hours or more continuity is not broken if you actually work fewer hours.

- Your contract does *not* have to lay down 16 hours or more a week *in writing*.
- Your contractual hours may be decided by reference to a collective agreement, company rules or custom and practice.

  - Joe Dean had been employed since 1971 as a barman in a social club. He worked the normal club opening hours and, if required, more hours. His contract said nothing about normal working hours. In 1976 he was made redundant. The EAT found that he qualified for a redundancy payment. In this kind of case, you have to look at what *actually* happened. In his last 104 weeks of employment, Joe Dean had worked 21 hours or more in 86 weeks and less than 21 hours in 18. Therefore, his contract normally involved working reckonable weeks which were then 21 hours or more per week (*Dean v Eastbourne Fishermen's Club* (1977) IRLR 143 EAT).

- Meal breaks do not count and overtime will only count if it is contractual and you are bound to work it. But if you *do* work it, it does count for that week.

- Your minimum laid down hours will *not* necessarily be your contractual hours. A part-time fireman who was on stand-by for 10½ hours a week was able to qualify even though he only averaged 10½ hours a week on actual duty (*Merseyside County Council v Bullock* (1979) IRLR 33 CA).
- Hours of work are counted even if some are unpaid, if they are required by the contract (*Graham v Minister of Labour* (1967) 2 ITR 162).
- A worker who does two jobs for the same employer can count the jobs together for the purpose of calculating the number of hours per week (*Birks v County of Armagh Education Committee* (1966) ITR 15 NI).

■ A worker who was sacked successfully appealed under a grievance procedure and was taken back. It was decided he had been suspended not sacked and continuity was not broken (*Howgate v Fane Acoustics Ltd* (1981) IRLR 161 EAT).

Contract for less than 16 hours a week

- If your contract is changed so that you are bound to work less than 16 hours but more than 8 hours a week, then weeks in which you work 8 hours or more will count towards total length of service and will not break continuity *provided* the 8–16 hour contractual weeks do not go beyond **26 weeks** in all before the original 16 hours or more a week are resumed under the contract. After that any legal rights to which you have become entitled by length of service are preserved.
- If you work under a contract which requires you to work 8 hours or more per week and if you accumulate **5 years** continuous employment, you will be entitled to the same rights as if you had worked 16 hours a week.
- If you work 8 hours but less than 16, it takes you **5 years** (not 1 year) to qualify for unfair dismissal, for example.

Temporary absence from work

If you are away from work but your contract of employment continues then the weeks that you are away *will* count in accumulating continuity of service according to the rules outlined above. This will apply if you are absent due to sickness, injury, pregnancy, holiday or temporary lay-off *provided* that your contract of employment is not terminated.

■ Jimmy Tarbuck was off work sick for nearly seven months. This counted towards the total length of his continuous employment. The employer could not produce any evidence to show that he had been sacked. John Thomson was absent for 16 months through illness. The period was included in calculating his length of continuous service. His contract had continued through his illness (*Tarbuck v Wilson Ltd* (1967) 2 ITR 157; *Thomson v Montieths Ltd* (1967) 2 ITR 205).

Temporary break in employment

If you resign from your job, or are sacked, and then a few weeks later you return, **you have to start completely afresh** in terms of building up continuity.

■ Jo McCann worked for almost 49 years for his boss. One day they got into an argument and Joe left and got a temporary job elsewhere. Shortly afterwards his boss asked him to come back with an increase in wages. He did, but nine months later was made redundant. He was not entitled to a statutory redundancy payment. Owing to the temporary break, his 49 years counted for nothing and he did not have 104 weeks continuous employment (*McCann v Andrew Miller Ltd* (1966) ITR 13 NI).

There are, however, exceptions to this rule if your contract is terminated in the following circumstances.

(1) *Sickness or injury*

If you are given notice when you are incapable of work because of sickness or injury, those weeks absent count and **continuity is not broken if you go back to work** and your absence has lasted no longer than 26 weeks.

(2) *Pregnancy*

The rule is the same as for sickness

(3) *Temporary cessation of work*

If you are sacked during a temporary cessation of work and you are later taken back, your weeks away count and **do not break continuity. You do not this time have to return within 26 weeks.** There are no strict guidelines laid down as to what a 'temporary stoppage' is. Absences of 2 years and 21 months have been held to be temporary absences which counted for continuity (*Bentley Engineering Ltd v Crown and Miller* (1976) IRLR 146 HC).

■ A teacher employed on a series of fixed term contracts did not have sufficient continuity because during the summer holidays each year she was not 'absent from work on account of a temporary cessation of work'. There was a gap between each yearly contract and continuity was broken (*Ford v Warwickshire County Council* (1982) IRLR 246 CA).

(4) *Arrangement or custom*

This situation is where you leave your job and your contract is legally terminated, but in reality it is expected that you will return at some point in the future. This might be so if your employer lent you to another company. **In this kind of situation your continuity is preserved**, your weeks away count and again there is no 26 weeks time limit set.

■ Taylor started at Triumph Motors on the staff side in 1957. To transfer to the shop floor he had to resign, join the relevant union and then apply for work under a collective agreement. He did this and returned to employment two months after resigning. A management/union agreement said: 'Length of continuous service shall be the length of continuous service with the specified group excepting that broken service up to a maximum of six months shall be calculated as continuous service'. The break was within the agreement which was an arrangement for the purposes of the law (*Taylor v Triumph Motors* (1975) IRLR 369).

It is essential, however, if your absence is to count, that **you establish some kind of arrangement or agreement**. (See *Corton House Ltd v Skipper* (1981) IRLR 78 EAT.)

(5) *Strikes and lock-outs*

If you are locked out by your employer, you cannot count the week **but it does not break your continuity.** If you are on strike, you cannot count the period of absence **but it does not break continuity. This applies to** *all strikes*, whatever the cause or category. You are also treated as not clocking up service yet not breaking continuity where you are employed outside GB without NI contributions being paid or where you return to your former boss within six months of a stint in the armed forces.

Change of employer

A change of employer does not break your continuity of employment if:

- the business you work for is **transferred** from one employer to another;
- if under an Act of Parliament one corporate body is **substituted** for another as your employer. (An example was the transfer of certain medical services from local authorities to the NAS in 1973);
- your boss **dies** and his personal representatives or trustees take you on;
- you are employed by a **partnership** and there is a change of partner;
- you go to work for another employer who at the time is an **associated employer**.

With takeovers there must be a transfer of the ownership of the business, trade, name, customers, good will. If all that is sold are the assets and the new business is quite different to the old, there *will* be a change of employment, and if you are later dismissed only service with the second employer will count (*Melon v Hector Powe* (1980) IRLR 477 HL). If you get a job with an employer who is an associated employer of your former employer then the two periods of employment count together and the change of employer does not count.

Two employers are associated if one is a company of which the other directly or indirectly has control or if both are companies of which a third person has control.

■ Jack Binns was made redundant by Versil Ltd after working for them for almost a year. He had previously worked for three years for Mintex Ltd, which he left off his own bat one Thursday. He started with Versil on the Monday, having seen a job with them advertised. Both companies were associated although neither company was aware that he had worked for the other. His employment with Mintex could be added to his employment with Versil so that he was entitled to a redundancy payment (*Binns v Versil Ltd* (1975) IRLR 273).

There may be complicated arguments as to whether two employers are associated or not. Recently a harder line has been taken.

The EAT has held that two employers are not associated unless one company owns 51 per cent of the shares of the other, or both are companies of which a third person owns 51 per cent of the shares (*Secretary of State for Employment v Newbould and Joint Liquidators of David Armstrong Catering Services Ltd* (1981) IRLR 305 EAT). The Court of Appeal has in effect overruled an earlier decision which held that two area health authorities in the same region were associated, so that service with one counted for continuity with the other (*Gardiner v London Borough of Merton* (1980) IRLR 472 CA).

The weeks a man worked while sponsored by the MSC under a work experience programme did not count when he was eventually taken on by the company itself (*Hawley v Fieldcastle* (1982) IRLR 223).

The length of your period of employment

Whether your employment with your boss is to be treated as forming a single period of continuous employment is to be calculated according to the rules we have looked at, laid down in EP(C)A sch. 13 week by week. But the *length* of your continuous employment is now under the 1982 Employment Act (s. 20 and sch. 2) to be computed in calendar months and years. Once a tribunal or court decide that you have an unbroken period of continuous employment, they will then switch to months and years to compute how long that period is.

Under the old rules you could count a whole week or part of a week in which you had a contract requiring you to work 16 hours or more. If you started work on Wednesday so long as your contract involved 16 hours or more over the whole week you could count back from Wednesday to Monday. The 1982 Act changes this so that the period begins with the day on which you start work. So if you start work on Wednesday you will no longer be able to count the entire week. For redundancy payments purposes your eighteenth birthday will be made the starting date if later than the first day you work. A period which does not count but does not break continuity is now calculated in terms of days not weeks. In a strike covering part of a week the whole week did not count. Now only the number of days between the start and the end of the strike will be lost. A period of continuous employment ends with the effective date of termination or the *relevant date* (see Chapter 4). If *this* falls on Wednesday you cannot count Thursday, Friday and Saturday.

These rules do not apply where the date on which your continuous service has to be worked out is before 2 January 1983 and they do not apply where you have built up sufficient continuous employment to qualify for a legal right under the old rules and would be deprived of that right because, for example, the dismissal takes place after January 1983 when the new rules apply.

Table 1: Your rights in industrial tribunals (continued)

Right	Time Limit	Service	Exclusions
1. Written statement of terms and conditions of employment. *Employment Protection (Consolidation) Act 1978* s.11	While at work or within 3 months from effective date of termination (EDT) of employment *EP(C)A* s. 11(9)	13 weeks	Central government employees *EP(C)A* s.138, registered dockers s.145(1), certain merchant seafarers 144(1), employees normally working abroad s.141(1)
2. Unfair dismissal *EP(C)A* s.67(1)	3 months from EDT. Maybe before EDT if dismissal with notice *EP(C)A* s.67(2)(4). Unfair selection of strikers for re-engagement: 6 months from applicant's date of dismissal *EA* 1982 s.9(5)	1 year. If your employer has less than 20 employees, 104 weeks *EP(C)A* s.64. *Employment Act 1980* s.8(1)	If you are over 60 (women), 65 (men) or normal retirement age for your job *EP(C)A* s.64(1), a share fisherman s.144(2), army or police 146(2), docker 145(2), or somebody who normally works abroad s.141(2). You must not be excluded under a designated dismissal procedure s.65 66
3. Written statement of reasons for dismissal *EP(C)A* s.53	3 months from EDT *EP(C)A* s.53(5)	6 months *EP(C)A* s.53(2). *EA 82* sch. 2(4)	See unfair dismissal
4. Redundancy payment *EP(C)A* s.91(1)	6 months from EDT *EP(C)A* s.101	2 years (service below age of 18 not counted) s.81(4)	See unfair dismissal but also if you do domestic work for a relative *EP(C)A* s.100(2), central government employees and some health service employees *EP(C)A* s.5, and oil rig workers, *Employment Protection Offshore Employment Order 1976; 1980*. Your job must not be subject to an exemption order *EP(C)A* s.96(1)

Right	Time Limit	Service	Exclusions
5. Breach of redundancy consultation. *Employment Protection Act 1975* s.101	Before dismissal or 3 months from EDT (union must take case) *EPA* s.101(6)	—	Dock workers *EPA* 119(3), merchant seafarers 119(12), employment outside GB 119(5), police, central government employees s.121, employees on fixed term contracts of 3 months or less and hired for job not expected to last for 3 months (unless it does *EPA* 119(7)). *EA 82* Sch. 2, 6(1)
6. Claim for remuneration under protective award *EPA* s.103	3 months from EDT s.103(2) (application by union)	—	As 5 above
7. Time off in redundancy situation *EP(C)A* s.31	3 months from refusal s.31(7)	2 years to date of expiry of notice	Army, police, share fishermen, dockers, merchant seafarers, employees working outside GB
8. Unfair selection for redundancy *EP(C)A* s.67(1)	3 months from EDT s.67(2)(4)	As 2 above	As 2 above
9. Victimisation for union membership or activities *EP(C)A* s.23	3 months from incident s.24(2)	—	As 7 above, but merchant seafarers and dockers not excluded
10. Dismissal for union membership or activities *EP(C)A* s.58	3 months from EDT s.67(2)(4) 7 days for interim procedure s.77(2)	—	As 2 above
11. Time off for union activities and duties *EP(C)A* s.27 28	3 months from date refused s.30(1)	—	As 9 above
12. Time off for public duties *EP(C)A* s.29	As 11 above	—	As 9 above, but merchant seafarers not covered

Your rights in industrial tribunals *(continued)*

Right	Time Limit	Service	Exclusions
13. Payment in insolvency *EP(C)A* s.124	3 months from Secretary of State's decision s.124(1)(2)	—	Same as 9 above, but central government employees are excluded
14. Itemised pay statement *EP(C)A* s.8	While working or within 3 months of leaving s.11(9), i.e. EDT	—	Armed forces, police, share fishermen, employees who ordinarily work outside GB, merchant seafarers
15. Guarantee payments *EP(C)A* s.12	3 months from due day s.17(2)	1 month s.13(1) sch. 2 *EA* s.2	Same as 14, but dock workers covered. Workers on fixed term contracts excluded as 5
16. Suspension on medical grounds *EP(C)A* s.22	3 months from due day s.22(2)	1 month s.20(1) *EA* sch. 2(2)	Same as 15 above
17. Sex discrimination, *Sex Discrimination Act 1975* s.63	3 months from discriminatory action *SDA* 76(1)	—	Work in private households, partnerships with less than 6 partners, armed forces, clergy, midwives, firms with less than 6 employees, *SDA* s.6, 11, 19, 20, 85 (and see s.7)
18. Race discrimination, *Race Relations Act 1976* s.54	3 months from action *RRA* s.68(1)(6)	—	Partnerships less than 6; employees in private households; seafarers recruited abroad *RRA* s.4, 9, 10
19. Equal pay, *Equal Pay Act 1970* s.2(1)	While working or within 6 months of leaving s.2(4)	6 months at date of reference	
20. Maternity pay *EP(C)A* s.36	3 months from due day	2 years at start of 11th week before expected date of confinement	Same as 9 above

Right	Time Limit	Service	Exclusions
21. Right to return to job after maternity leave (claim for unfair dismissal or redundancy payment)	As 2, 4 above	As 20 above	As 2, 4 above
22. Time off for ante-natal care *EP(C)A s.31 by Employment Act 1980*	3 months from refusal	—	
23. Unfair exclusion or expulsion from union *Employment Act 1980 s.4*	Initial application, six months from date of expulsion or exclusion. For compensation, as soon as 4 weeks up to 6 months after date of declaration *EA s.4(6) s.5(3)*	—	As 10 above
24. Information and consultation on transfer of enterprise, transfer of undertakings *(Protection of Employment) Regulations 1981, Reg 10, 11*	3 months from date of relevant transfer para 11(8) Recognised union applies	—	*Registered Dockworkers, Reg 13*
25. Occupational pensions, right of union to be consulted *Occupational Pension Schemes Regulations 1975 Reg 4*	None	—	—
Equal Access for men and women *OPSR 1976 Reg 12*	—	—	—
Unpaid contributions in insolvency *EP(C)A s.123,124*	3 months from Secretary of State's Decision	—	—

Note: Abbreviations used in this table: **EA82** = Employment Act 1982; **EDT** = Effective Date of Termination; **EPA** = Employment Protection Act 1975; **EP(C)A** = Employment Protection (Consolidation) Act 1978; **SDA** = Sex Discrimination Act 1975; **RRA** = Race Relations Act 1976.

4.

Time limits for tribunal cases

When parliament gives people legal rights, it normally lays down time limits within which each legal right must be used. After a specified time your right becomes statute barred and you cannot take the matter to court. In the same way, **if you do not get your application for a tribunal hearing in time, you will be disqualified**. So after you have worked out (from Chapter 2) that you are entitled to take a case, you must ensure that you apply to a tribunal in time. You can see the different time limits in Table 1. This chapter looks in detail at these time limits, how they have been interpreted, and some of the pitfalls you must avoid to ensure a hearing.

Where to find the law
See Table 1, EP(C)A s. 49, s. 55(4)(5) 67 90.

Unfair dismissal

You *can* present a case to an industrial tribunal *during* the statutory minimum period of notice that you are entitled to from your employer.

You *must* do so:

- **within three months** of the effective date of termination of your contract; or
- within such further period outside these three months as the tribunal considers reasonable; because it was **not reasonably practicable** for the complaint to be presented within the three months.

The time limit during which you *have* to bring a case runs from the effective date of termination.

Unlike the time limits on some other legal actions, this rule is fundamental to the jurisdiction of the tribunal. If its requirements are not met then the tribunal *cannot* hear the case. The employer *cannot* agree to waive the rule (*Westward Circuits v Read* (1973) IRLR 138 NIRC).

When does the three months start?

The effective date of termination establishes when your period of continuous employment with your employer ends. This date is *vital* in establishing:

- whether you have worked continuously for the 52 weeks or 104 weeks (small firms) required to qualify for unfair dismissal, or the two years required to qualify for a legal redundancy payment;
- what your period of continuous employment is, for computing the various sums of compensation that you are entitled to if you win your case; for example, the number of years you have worked with the employer affects any redundancy payment;
- whether your claim has been presented within the time limit allowed for presenting cases to a tribunal.

The effective date of termination may be different according to how you are sacked. There may be at least five different situations.

(1) **Dismissal with proper notice where the worker works out the notice:** In this case there will be no problem and the effective date of termination will be the date the notice runs out.

(2) **The worker is employed under a contract for a fixed time period:** When that time period expires then the date of expiry will be the effective date of termination.

(3) **Dismissal without notice:** If the worker is sacked without notice and leaves work then the date of the sacking will be the effective date of termination for the purpose of the time limit even though the worker was in fact entitled to a longer period of contractual or statutory notice. However, for the purposes of calculating the worker's period of continuous service for qualification for various legal rights and computation of compensation, the effective date of termination will be the end of the statutory period of notice to which the worker would be entitled under the EP(C)A.

The effective date of termination in this situation will be the date of actual dismissal even if the worker is given wages in lieu of notice. 'If a man is dismissed without notice but with money in lieu what he receives is a matter of law damages for breach of contract. During the period to which the money in lieu of notice applies he is not employed by his employer.' (*Dixon v Stenor Ltd* (1973) IRLR 28 NIRC).

■ On 5 May 1972 Ron Dedman, a contracts manager, was given a letter from his employers sacking him immediately. He left the premises handing over his car, his keys and other company property. He was paid for the full month of May and given one month's pay in lieu of notice. He knew that he had some right to claim unfair dismissal but not that there was a time limit. There was an argument as to whether his dismissal was out of time. The CA held that the effective date of termination from which you calculated the time limit was the date he received the letter, whether the dismissal was in fact fair or unfair (*Dedman v British Building and Engineering Appliances Ltd* (1973) IRLR 379 CA).

There may be an exception where an employer gives notice of dismissal and then tries to bring the notice period to an end by asking the worker to leave work *before* the end of the notice period with full pay in lieu. In the case of *Brindle v Smith (Cabinets) Ltd* (1973) 1 AER 230 CA, an employer initially gave a worker a week's notice and then tried to sack the worker before the period elapsed. The Court of Appeal held that dismissal did not take place until the due notice had expired even though the notice had in fact been reduced. In such cases the effective date of termination will be the last day of the full contractual period of notice. But if a worker leaves earlier by mutual agreement, that agreement date will be the effective date.

(4) **The worker has been given notice by the employer and gives the employer counter-notice that she or he intends to leave earlier:** In this kind of situation the effective date of termination will be the date that the worker's counter-notice expires and he or she *leaves*, rather than the date that the employer's original notice ends.

(5) **The worker claims that the employer's fundamental breach of contract has left him or her with no alternative but to leave employment:** In other words, the constructive dismissal situation. The effective date of dismissal here has not been clearly defined in statute or case law. However, the comments of the Court of Appeal in the case of *Western Excavating (ECC) Ltd v Sharp* (1978) IRLR 27 CA suggest that it is the action of the worker in

leaving rather than the employer's behaviour which brings the contract to an end. Therefore, if the worker leaves without notice, the date she or he leaves is likely to be the effective date of termination. If the worker leaves after giving notice then the effective date of termination would seem to be the end of that notice period. In unfair dismissal cases the effective date of termination for the purpose of calculating continuous service will be the end of the statutory period of notice to which the employee would be entitled to receive from the employer.

If you are sacked by letter the EDT will be not when the letter is sent but when you receive it or when you might reasonably be expected to have received it (*Brown v Southall & Knight* (1980) IRLR 130 EAT).

Appeals

Where workers are sacked but given a right of appeal, is the effective date of termination the date of the dismissal or the date of the appeal (where the appeal is unsuccessful)? The answer will depend on an interpretation of the contract, the appeals procedure and the behaviour of the employer and worker. Where a letter of dismissal stated 'your dismissal will take effect from the end of today's working day and all sums due to you will be forwarded to you in due course with all relevant documents', it was held that the date of the letter, not the date of the rejection of an appeal, was the effective date of termination (*McDonald v South Cambridgeshire* RDC (1973) IRLR 308 NIRC). This approach has been confirmed by the Court of Appeal (*J. Sainsbury Ltd v Savage AC* (1980) IRLR 109 CA) but the result of this test may not be the same in every case. The tribunal should look at the intention of the parties and the details of the contract.

■ Messrs King and Grant were dismissed on 13 September 1978 by Schweppes for serious misconduct. They appealed through three stages of the procedure, and on 18 January 1979 their appeal was rejected and dismissal confirmed on 26 January. They claimed unfair dismissal in April 1979 and the company argued that as their complaints were outside the time limit the case should not be heard. The date of dismissal, King and Grant argued, was 26 January not 13 September 1978. The workers' argument was upheld by the tribunal, whereas in the Sainsbury case the worker understood that he was dismissed, claimed unemployment benefit and was removed from the salary roll; the workers in this case had remained on full pay until the January date and the Schweppes rules stated: 'In the event of an appeal dismissal will not take effect until the appeal has been heard' (*King and Grant v Schweppes* COIT No 926/43).

The same kind of approach will be taken where a worker *successfully* appeals against a decision to dismiss. If the contract provides for a right of appeal, indicating that the contract remains in being, if only for the limited purpose of exercising the right of appeal, then the effective date of termination will be the later date. Therefore, in a case where a transfer was substituted for the sack as a result of a successful appeal but the worker found the new job unacceptable, the effective date of termination is the date the worker finally leaves and the time limit runs from then.

If you are claiming 'action short of dismissal' has been taken against you, the time limit runs from the moment you are told your appeal against that action has failed, not the moment when that action was initially taken (*British Airways Board v Clark & Havill* (1982) IRLR 461 EAT).

When does the period end?

The three months are calendar months (Interpretation Act 1978 Schedule 1). In calculating the three months, the actual day of dismissal is counted and so **the period will run out the day before the equivalent date three months ahead** (*Hammond v Haigh Castle* (1973) IRLR 91; *Reeves v Marley Tile* (1975) 10 ITR 192; *Boyd v CWS Furnishing Group Ltd* (1982) EAT 68/82). If you are effectively sacked on 12 December, then the last day you can present your case to the tribunal is 11 March.

When is a case presented to a tribunal?

In the case of *Hammond v Haigh Castle* (1973) IRLR 91 NIRC, the court said:

In our judgement a claim is presented to a tribunal when it is received by the tribunal whether or not it is dealt with immediately upon receipt. Thus a claim delivered to a tribunal office by post on Saturday is presented on that day even if not registered before the following Monday. A claim is not, however, presented by the act of posting it addressed to the tribunal.

- Mr Gardiner was sacked on 7 August 1972. On Friday 1 September he sent an originating application claiming unfair dismissal by post to the Central Office of Tribunals. His application was not delivered until Monday 4 September 1972. The time limit expired at midnight on Sunday 3 March. The NIRC held that Gardiner's application was presented in time. As the date of expiry of the time limit was a Sunday, it was sufficient that the application was delivered to the office on the next working day (*Anglo-Continental School of English (Bournemouth) Ltd v Gardiner* (1973) 8 ITR 251 NIRC).

The EAT have now held, however (in *Hetton Victory Club Ltd v Swainston* (1982) EAT 196/82) that, **where the time limit expires on a non-working day, the complaint must be presented on that day and the time limit cannot be treated as expiring on the next working day**. The position is different in the Six Counties, where the time limit can be extended (Interpretation (NI) Act (1954 s. 39)).

If you send your application by first class post, reasonably expecting that it will arrive at the Central Office of Industrial Tribunals the following day, and it does not, then, if you have a time limit problem, you can argue that it was not reasonably practicable for you to get your application in within the three months and that you did so within a reasonable time afterwards.

- Jack Burton delayed making a complaint of unfair dismissal against his employer as his application for an alternative job with that employer was still being considered by the company and he did not want to prejudice his chances. On Thursday 22 January 1976 he posted his application off first class recorded delivery but it did not arrive until Monday 26 January, three days out of time. The tribunal held that, as he had deliberately delayed making his application, it *was* reasonably practicable for Burton to have presented his claim within three months. The Appeals Tribunal then held that Burton *was* entitled to delay in the circumstances and that provided he posted it within the time limit period, so that in the normal course of post and except for unforeseen circumstances, it would have been received in time, then a tribunal ought to find that it was not reasonably practicable for the complaint to have been presented within the three months and the case should be heard (*Burton v Field* (1977) ICR 106 EAT).

Not reasonably practicable

If your application is received by the tribunal outside the time limit then you have to argue that you fall within this escape clause. The onus of proof is on you.

The basic question is, have you got a good reason or excuse for not presenting your case within three months? Can you show that you have been extremely sick because of your dismissal, suffered from acute stress or nervous illness, or that some unexpected event or emergency has made it very difficult for you to apply within three months?

- For example, a worker was able to have the time limit extended when, after his dismissal, his father was taken ill and died. The worker was pre-occupied with family responsibilities and the problems of the funeral (*Pesticcio v British Steel Corporation* (1973) 2934/73).

- Mrs McKeown was sacked by Tesco on 9 March 1978 as the management suspected her of stealing from the shop she worked in. She was in a distraught state after her dismissal and her doctor prescribed valium. A tribunal held that despite the fact that her application was presented some seven weeks out of time, they had discretion to hear her case. Her mental state meant that it had not been reasonably practicable for her to comply with the time limit. At the hearing itself she was unable to recollect dates or make a coherent statement. Moreover, she had been away from work for six months because of a nervous complaint and had returned only four days before the alleged offence. The tribunal decision was upheld by the EAT (*Tesco Stores Ltd v McKeown* (1978) EAT 78/719).

- In another case, a worker knew that he had a right to claim unfair dismissal and that there was a time limit. He thought, however, that his appeal to a national insurance tribunal about unemployment benefit was his industrial tribunal claim. He was confused by the use of the term 'tribunal', thought that the insurance tribunal would in fact hear his claim for unfair dismissal, and realised his mistake only at the unemployment hearing. It was held that the mistake was genuine and one which in the circumstances, since the worker was from Bangladesh, was understandable. The mistake made it not reasonably practicable for him to apply within the time limit. When he discovered his mistake he applied as quickly as possible (*Walls Meat Co. v Khan* (1979) IRLR 499 CA).

The other main argument that workers have put forward has been ignorance of the law or its details. The broad test is, was the worker's ignorance justifiable and acceptable or not? More specifically, as Lord Denning said in one case:

If in the circumstances the man knew or was put on inquiry as to his rights and as to the time limit then it was 'practicable' for him to have presented his complaint within the time limit and he ought to have done so but if he did not know and there was nothing to put him on inquiry then it was not practicable and he should be excused (*Dedman v British Building & Engineering Appliances Ltd* (1973) IRLR 379 CA).

You cannot get through the loophole simply by showing that you didn't know the law. You have to show that you could not reasonably be expected to have been aware of the true position, that there was no reason why you should have inquired further. You are 'put on inquiry' if you are given government booklets about unfair dismissal or if you know that there is a time limit but do not know how long it is. You are expected to find out and act on what you have discovered.

■ Mrs O'Regan worked for Times Newspapers. She was sacked on 12 June 1975. Her union officials were then involved in negotiations with the management on her behalf, first to try to get her job back and then for a favourable reference. She discussed the question of unfair dismissal proceedings with her official but whilst she knew that there *was* a time limit, she thought that the time limit ran from the end of negotiations, not from the date of the sacking itself. When negotiations broke down in October she filed an unfair dismissal application. The tribunal found that it *was* reasonably practicable for her to have brought her case within the three months and the EAT agreed. She knew that there was a time limit and that it was three months. She was under a duty to make inquiries in order to confirm the date from which it ran. She had no just cause or excuse for not bringing the case within the three month period (*Times Newspapers v O'Regan* (1977) IRLR 101 EAT).

Tribunals have been told to 'be astute in considering the explanation that may be given by an applicant who is out of time' (*Thomas v William H. Capper & Co. Ltd* (1979) EAT 619/79). It will be very difficult today for workers to convince a tribunal that they do not know about the legal right to take an unfair dismissal case to a tribunal.

■ A worker recently attempted to convince the courts that he did not know of the existence of the unfair dismissal remedy or the time limit until 11 months after he had been sacked, when he was told by his shop steward that he had a right to take tribunal proceedings. The majority of the Court of Appeal upheld a tribunal decision that he was not entitled to take a case. They felt that after eight years of well publicised activities by tribunals in unfair dismissal cases, it was not reasonable for a worker not to have known of his or her right or to have taken 11 months to find out.

Lord Ormerod dissented, however. He felt that the time limit should be strictly construed since it is very short in comparison with other limitation periods and those affected are ordinary workers. If you know of your remedy, he said, you can be expected as a reasonable person to make inquiries on how to obtain it. There can be no duty to make inquiries about the existence of a remedy of which you are unaware (*Porter v Bandridge* (1978) IRLR 271 CA).

Liability of union officials and advisers

Lord Denning said in the Dedman case, 'If a man engages skilled advisers to act for him and they mistake the time limits and present it too late – he is out. His remedy is against them.' In some cases it was held that as well as solicitors or Citizens Advice Bureaux, union officials – even convenors – were skilled advisers (*Syed v Ford Motor Co.* (1979) IRLR 335).

In a recent case, however, the Court of Appeal stated that consulting unskilled or skilled advisers is not material to the question of applying in reasonably practicable time. The question to be decided is whether the worker or adviser, unskilled or skilled, is at fault. If either is at fault or unreasonable then it would be reasonably practicable for the complaint to be presented in time (*Riley v Tesco Stores Ltd* (1980) IRLR 103 CA).

Whether an adviser is at fault and can be sued when the

tribunal turn down the case is always a question of fact and past precedents will be of little value. However, it is clear that if a union full-time or lay official fails to advise a member on a relevant matter, such as time limits, or incorrectly advises the member, then the tribunal may find the case is barred and refer the member for compensation to an action against the official. **Representatives have to be scrupulously careful here. If you are advising on a possible tribunal case, ask yourself: what time limits apply?** (But see page 65.)

Remember also the point about appeals. In some cases, tribunals may decide that the time limit runs from the date of initial dismissal, not from the date of decision on the appeal. The adviser should clarify the situation so that: (a) it is agreed that dismissal will operate only from rejection of appeal, or (b) put the case in at the time of initial dismissal which, of course, may influence the appeal.

If the mistake about the time limit is the employer's fault a case may not be time barred. Where a manager specifically asked the worker not to take a case to a tribunal until the internal appeal had been heard, it was decided that the worker's reliance on this statement made it not practicable for the application to have been made in time (*Owen v Crown House Engineering Ltd* (1973) 3 AER 618 (1973) IRLR 233 NIRC).

Interim relief

If you have been dismissed for **a reason connected with trade-union membership or activities**, you may apply to a tribunal for an interim remedy under a special emergency procedure. You must show that you are 'likely to succeed' at the full hearing. If you do, you will be entitled to a tribunal order which basically means that you are suspended on full pay.

This kind of application has to be made **within seven days of the effective date of termination**. It has to be accompanied by a certificate in writing signed by an authorised official of the union, stating that the official has reasonable grounds for believing that the principal reason for dismissal was union membership or activities. The time limit is very short and **there is no escape clause. If the application falls outside the seven days, the case cannot be heard.** It is rare for a case to be heard outside the limit.

■ Twelve workers were sacked on 30 July: eight wrote letters to the tribunal on 3 or 4 August, as the seven days time limit expired on 6 August. These applications did not refer to the relevant sections of the act, nor did they state that the reason for the dismissal was 'trade-union activities'. They did use the words 'interim relief'. The other four applications were not received until after 6 August. On 11 August, the union submitted a detailed letter. The EAT overruling the tribunal decided that the cases could be heard. Whilst an important principle here was speed 'and we are not to be taken as saying that however late the later applications are the applicant is entitled as of right to have them read together. We think that there must be a discretion.' Moreover the four applications submitted later than the time limit were associated with the others (*Barley v Amey Roadstone Corporation Ltd* (1977) ICR 546 EAT).

Unfair dismissal of strikers

If you are claiming unfair dismissal because your ex-employer was 'picking and choosing' by taking back any of the workers involved in the industrial action but not others, then you have **six months from the date of your dismissal** to apply to a tribunal. For example, if two months after everybody on strike is sacked the employers offer to re-engage one of the strikers, the rest still have four months in which to bring their case.

'Date of dismissal' in these cases is the date when notice is given to you, not the date when that notice expires.

Redundancy payments

Much of what has been said about unfair dismissal goes here. However, there are some important differences.

To receive redundancy payment, the worker must show that, **within six months from the relevant date**:

- the payment has been agreed and paid; or
- a claim for the payment has been made in writing to the employer; or
- a complaint about the right to the payment or about the amount of the payment has been made to an industrial tribunal; or
- a complaint of unfair dismissal has been filed with an industrial tribunal.

missal was, and that she or he acted reasonably. It is important to scrutinise this on the IT3. Sometimes the employer will plead in the alternative:

■ In one important case, the employers gave as their reason for dismissal: '(a) redundancy and/or (b) the incapability of the employee for performing work of the kind which he was employed by the employer to do.' On the facts of the case there was no redundancy situation in law but the tribunal were able to identify capability (*Abernethy v Mott Hay and Anderson* (1974) IRLR 213 (1974) ICR 323 CA).

Where the employer has given an incorrect legal reason for dismissal on the IT3 then there is still a chance to amend the form at the hearing on the lines that we have described for the workers' side.

A tribunal can refuse to allow amendment of an IT3 if it would cause unfairness to the applicant (*Kapur v Shields* (1976) ICR 26 HC). Amendment may also be refused if it would change the basis of the case if requested at a late stage, and if the employer has had professional advice, a request to amend may be turned down (*Ready Case v Jackson* (1981) IRLR 312).

An employer who does not ask for amendment may be in trouble.

■ David Nelson worked for the BBC Caribbean Service. He was sacked after the BBC closed the service down and they claimed before the tribunal that he was redundant. The tribunal accepted this but the EAT found that his work was not limited to the Caribbean Service so that the dismissal could not be redundancy. They however accepted the suggestion made for the first time that the dismissal was for 'some other substantial reason'. The Court of Appeal said that this was wrong. Redundancy was the only defence pleaded before the tribunal and no application to amend that defence had been made (*Nelson v BBC* (1977) ICR 649 CA).

Tribunals *cannot* find that the reason for dismissal is a reason that the employer has not stated. If the employer does not request amendment and the tribunal *do* this without allowing an adjournment to enable you to deal properly with the new issue, **you can challenge the decision**.

Preliminary hearings

Preliminary hearings are usually held to sort out a jurisdictional problem, like has the worker 52 weeks continuous employment? Is the case out of time?

Preliminary hearings can save the time and expense of both sides preparing a case which may fall at the first hurdle.

The hearing will sort out this basic jursidictional point, on which further proceedings hinge. A full hearing will then take place on the merits of the case *if* the tribunal decides it has jurisdiction to hear it. It is normally the employer who will ask for a preliminary hearing, but you can – and so can the tribunal.

The procedure is the same as for a full hearing. You may want to argue that a preliminary hearing should not take place as the issue cannot be settled without going into the merits of the case. For example, to decide whether the worker was constructively dismissed would involve delving into the whole circumstances of the case. The EAT have stated that preliminary hearings should not be held where they will simply duplicate hearings to take place later and *increase*, not save, time and expenses (*Meghani v Career Care Group Ltd* (1979) EAT 772/78), or where the tribunal in a preliminary hearing will have to come to a conclusion on legal points which can be decided only by assuming certain facts which may later turn out to be incorrect (*Turley v Allders Department Stores Ltd* (1980) ICR 66 EAT).

Pre-hearing assessments

Despite the process of vetting and the possibility of preliminary hearing, employers have long claimed that the tribunals allow through to a hearing too many cases which have no chance of succeeding and which subject them to needless time and expense. There is no evidence of this, but Tory legislation is based on myth, not reality. The 1980 Tribunal Regulations attempt to make the worker's path to a hearing more difficult and to discourage applications by introducing pre-hearing assessments. This means that now a tribunal will not merely consider whether or not it has jurisdiction to hear the worker's case. The tribunal will also look at the substance and merits of the case to see whether it has a reasonable prospect of success.

It will generally be employers who will use this mechanism, but either side may ask for a pre-hearing by writing to the secretary of tribunals, or the chairperson can initiate such an assessment. Cases selected for a pre-hearing assessment will be those where the chairperson considers, on the basis of the written documents, that possibly one side or the other has no case. You will be informed and your arguments will be heard by a full tribunal in private. If the tribunal decides that your case is unlikely to succeed or that your contentions have no reasonable prospect of success, they will let you know that if you pursue the case you may have costs awarded against you at the full hearing if your case is unsuccessful.

The tribunal's 'indication of opinion' will be registered in a certificate and will be made available to the tribunal which hears the full case, if you decide to pursue the case against the tribunal's advice. This later tribunal will be differently constituted. To avoid it being influenced by the opinion of the first, this certificate will be available to the second tribunal in a sealed envelope. It will be opened only at the end of the case, if you are not successful.

- The tribunal must give notice to both sides of the assessment and give them the opportunity to submit written representations.
- The other party to the case is entitled to attend, but tribunals may indicate that this is not necessary.
- No witnesses or verbal evidence will be heard, but either side may be accompanied by a representative if they wish.
- The hearing will centre around the contents of the IT1 and IT3 and any other written submissions.

As well as discouraging applicants, this new provision could lead to longer delays.

From October 1980 to October 1981, 1,778 assessments were ordered: 19 initiated by workers; 984 by the tribunal; 286 cases were settled or withdrawn before the PHA. In 699 of the cases heard, warnings about costs were given against the worker. In 12 cases, the employer was warned; 541 cases were withdrawn after the costs warning. Of the cases which went to a full hearing, the worker lost 107, or 83 per cent. Costs were awarded against the worker in 37, or 31 per cent, of the cases. So you can see that the tribunals are not automatically awarding costs.

Remember: No reasons are given for the decision at an assessment and there is no appeal (*Mackie v John Holt Vintners Ltd* (1982) IRLR 236 EAT).

If your case *is* going forward, it is allocated to the relevant regional office – the region in which the events you are complaining about took place. The application then goes to the registration section where it is entered on the register, which is open for public inspection, and is given a case number to be used in all future correspondence. The IT1 is then sent to the regional office and the central office is then generally not involved again, until the decision is sent to it by the regional office to be entered on the register with the initial particulars.

Conciliation and settlement

When your employer knows that you have started a tribunal case, she or he may be willing to consider negotiating a settlement with you rather than let the case go to a hearing. Unless you have some wider objective, such as using a hearing to publicise a particular situation, you will obviously want to consider any offers.

In order to encourage employers and workers to settle problems themselves and limit the workload of tribunals, the law also provides for a conciliation process to be built into the tribunal procedure. This procedure applies to most of the employment rights but not to claims for statutory redundancy payment.

Where to find the law
EP(C)A s.133, s.134, s.140
EPA s.108, s.118
SDA s.64, s.77
RRA s.55, s.72
Industrial Tribunal Regulations 2(1), 2(4), 11(2)(a), (b), (c), (d)

Conciliation

A copy of your form IT1 and the employer's reply, IT3 are sent to the regional ACAS office for your particular area. They are then passed on to a conciliation officer. ACAS may have been involved in your case under their general industrial relations duties before you applied to an industrial tribunal. They can get involved if either side asks *before* an application is made to a tribunal. They will, however, be involved again, dealing with the case specifically in the context of the tribunal complaint.

However, it is not an *absolute requirement* in all circumstances that the relevant documents be sent to the conciliation officer. In certain cases the fact that this officer has not been involved will not necessarily mean that a tribunal decision is null and void (*Sheringham Development Co. Ltd v Browne* (1977) ICR 20 EAT).

The job of the conciliation officer is to see if the case can be settled without the necessity for a tribunal hearing.

The conciliation officer has a legal duty to take action if he or she is:

(a) asked to do so by *both* sides in the case; or
(b) not asked to do so but is of the view that he or she could act with a reasonable prospect of success.

In practice, when an officer receives the tribunal forms, he or she does not wait for the parties to get in touch or for a date to be fixed for a tribunal hearing. Rather, the officer takes the initiative and gets in touch with both sides right away assuming automatically that there is a reasonable prospect of success in dealing with the case. The officer will explain the position to both parties and offer conciliation. However, if your side or the employer's side is unwilling to accept conciliation, the officer simply informs the other side and the matter is left there. It will then go forward to a hearing.

What is conciliation?

ACAS distinguish three processes in their work:

(1) **Arbitration** – a process by which a problem, on which unions and management cannot agree, is submitted to an outsider who will generally conduct a hearing, find the facts and make a judgement.

(2) **Conciliation** – the job of ACAS is to bring the parties together, to attempt to get them talking and to act as a lubricant in re-establishing a negotiation relationship. The conciliator can act as a go-between and help to clarify the situation but should encourage the parties to find a solution *themselves*, not impose an external ready-made solution. Conciliation involves kick-starting and then orchestrating the collective bargaining process.

(3) **Mediation** – a similar process to conciliation but involving the outsider more deeply. Here, the officer will not merely be trying to bring the parties together and get them talking but will make his or her own formal detailed proposals or recommendations, which the parties may find acceptable or on which they may negotiate further. Mediation is a halfway house between arbitration and conciliation.

Conciliation officers should explain their role to each side pointing out that they are not acting as fact finders for the tribunal or as representatives for union or management. The conciliation process is extremely informal and it is difficult to generalise.

The first step is normally a separate brief discussion between the officer and each side. The conciliator will be looking for basic information on the facts of the dispute and your attitude to your case and a possible settlement. She or he may also ask for copies of documents.

The officer may then ask you to attend a joint meeting with the employer, which may involve a joint dicussion. The officer will make an introductory statement, and then you and the employer can state your position. The meeting will then go into questions and discussion. At some stage the officer may leave the parties together to try to hammer out a solution. **If you are involved with conciliation, remember:**

(1) the officer has the duty at all stages to consider whether other procedures than a tribunal hearing would help to settle the case. If an employer has not followed an industrial relations procedure which you think would help your case, you should point this out to the officer and try to enlist ACAS's support;

(2) in dismissal cases the officer has a specific duty to promote the reinstatement or re-engagement of the worker *before* talking about compensation. If the employer is reluctant to discuss reinstatement, you should point out to the officer that it is his or her statutory duty to focus on this matter *first*, and to ensure that this possibility is rigorously discussed. If the discussion then moves to compensation, the figures discussed should include a factor for the employer's refusal to reinstate;

(3) if the case is being handled by a full-time official or shop steward, then the conciliation officer will deal with them. There is nothing to stop the member being present however, and in many situations it will be best for *both* to be involved in the conciliation process;

(4) anything either side says to a conciliation officer cannot be brought up as evidence before the tribunal *unless* that party gives their permission. The idea is that if conciliation is to be successful and involve either side in moving from their initial position, then it has to involve frank talking and therefore confidentiality. If their statements could be brought up before the tribunal, both sides would simply clam up. So if an employer says, 'I have been

trying to find a chance to sack him for the last two years' to a conciliation officer, you will not be able to bring this as evidence before the tribunal or get the officer to appear as a witness. Offers of compensation made during conciliation cannot be disclosed to the tribunal unless both sides agree.

The same applies to documents specifically prepared for the conciliation process. You cannot, however, simply give all your documentation, copies of warnings and disciplinary letters to the conciliation officer and then claim that this material is privileged and cannot be produced before the tribunal or disclosed to the other party.

■ The company gave copies of minutes of a meeting between management and shop stewards held before the dismissal and copies of internal management memos to the conciliation officer. They then claimed that these documents were now privileged and could not, therefore, be disclosed to the sacked worker or be produced before the tribunal. The NIRC decided that the minutes were subject to the general rules on discovery (see page 136) and the memos would only be protected if they were drawn up *specifically* for the purpose of achieving a settlement (*Grazebrook Ltd v Wallens* (1973) 8 ITR 258 NIRC).

(5) Conciliation can take place at any stage of tribunal procedure – even during the actual hearing of the case. The tribunals often feel that a voluntary agreement is more satisfactory than one they have imposed, and will adjourn up to a decision and even afterwards for discussion of compensation.

Role of the conciliation officer

The 1976 ACAS Annual Report states that the officer

tries to help the parties to reach an agreement but he does not act as an arbitrator on the merits of the case, nor does he impose or even recommend a particular settlement . . . it is not part of his role to persuade or cajole parties to settle. Settlements are the responsibility of the parties concerned.

You have to remember at all times that, according to the rules, the conciliation officer is simply there as a channel of information, a stimulator attempting to prod the two sides into coming to their own agreement.

ACAS go on to say:

> he cannot allow his own views of the merits of the case to intrude . . If either party asks a question such as 'How good is my case?' or 'What are my chances at the tribunal?' he cannot give a direct answer. He can however draw their attention to relevant precedents . . . they would be failing in their responsibilities to some complainants if they did not draw their attention to qualifying conditions, case law and precedent, the strong points in the respondent's case and to the risk of costs being awarded if the tribunal considers either party has acted in a frivolous or vexatious fashion. However, it would be quite improper for a conciliation officer to indicate that in his opinion action by either party was frivolous or vexatious as only a tribunal can form a view on this.

The theory is that, while the officer can make general points about the case, you have to draw your own conclusions. You should not *rely* on anything the officer may tell you. In the end you have to make up your own mind. Do *not* think that if an officer does not object to a settlement it is reasonable or even in line with comparable tribunal decisions.

Many people who have experience of conciliation will tell you that the conciliation officer seems to go beyond the function ACAS lays down and in some cases has specifically advised them to accept a settlement or to make an offer, or has commented on the chances of success or failure of the specific case that is being dealt with.

Be clear: **you are not under any obligation to accept this kind of advice** nor should you feel any pressure to do so.

If the advice is incorrect or misguided, *you* may lose out. Listen carefully to conciliation officers but always check independently before accepting their views.

Remember: Like any professional, an officer wants to be good at the job. The settlement rate may be seen as the yardstick of a good conciliation officer, and this may lead an officer to push for settlement when it may be in your interest to refuse.

In a recent survey over two-thirds of applicants who obtained a settlement or won their case at an industrial tribunal, said that they found the conciliation officer helpful. However, only a quarter of those who lost their case or withdrew without settlement felt that the conciliation officer had been helpful.

Employers who settled generally thought that ACAS had been helpful whilst those who went on to a hearing did not. The survey showed that 39 per cent of workers and 46 per cent of employers thought the officer had given them advice and 48 per cent of these workers and 68 per cent of these employers claimed to have received advice which went beyond the officer's role. For example, 26 per cent and 59 per cent of these workers and employers respectively claimed that they were told to settle/accept or make an offer/drop the case. Whilst this may sometimes be a matter of how the parties interpret the officers' statements it is clear that specific advice *is* often given. (Linda Dickens, 'Unfair Dismissal Applications and the Industrial Tribunal System', *Department of Employment Gazette*, March 1979.)

Forms

If you are involved in a settlement the conciliation officer will get the parties to fill in the relevant ACAS forms registering the decision. These are:

- **COT2:** settlement with re-engagement and/or compensation;
- **COT3:** settlement with details of cash and any other statements as to responsibilities etc; and
- **COT4:** withdrawal of case by the applicant.

Settlements

What is your *objective* in taking the case? If you want compensation or reinstatement, negotiation will be worthwhile though the latter is rarely achieved. If you are interested in your reputation, a statement and reference may be agreed, though most settlements state that the employer does not accept liability. If you want to publicly clear your name or air a grievance it may be a bad idea to settle.

Obviously before any settlement is accepted, workers and representatives need to consider what is on offer in relation to the strength of the case, the chances of success, the chances of reinstatement and the going rate of compensation in similar cases. You will generally no longer have your most important bargaining weapon – the possibility of industrial sanctions. However, you should still consider the employer's position.

ADVISORY CONCILIATION AND ARBITRATION SERVICE

* Equal Pay Act 1970
* Sex Discrimination Act 1975
* Race Relations Act 1976
* Employment Protection Act 1975
* Employment Protection (Consolidation) Act 1978
* Employment Act 1980
* Employment Act 1982
* AGREEMENT IN RESPECT OF AN APPLICATION MADE TO THE INDUSTRIAL TRIBUNAL

* AGREEMENT IN RESPECT OF A REQUEST FOR CONCILIATION MADE TO THE ADVISORY CONCILIATION & ARBITRATION SERVICE (NO APPLICATION MADE TO TRIBUNAL AT TIME OF AGREEMENT)

Tribunal case number

....

Applicant	Respondent
Name	Name ....
Address	Address ....
....	....

Settlement reached as a result of conciliation action.

We the undersigned have agreed:

Applicant .... date...............

Respondent... date...............

* Delete inappropriate item

0593483 10M 11/82 AP Ltd

Form COT3

- Is he or she hesitant about proceeding to the tribunal because of publicity?
- Might the case highlight dubious employment practices?
- Is the case likely to cause tension and problems with other employees – particularly if they are to be called as witnesses?
- Is the employer worried that a voluntary settlement may set a precedent which will lead to a number of other claims?
- What is the overall cost of the case in terms of money, time and inconvenience likely to be in relation to the cost of settling now?

If you are considering a financial settlement, you should prepare your case for compensation before the tribunal in full detail (see Chapter 12), assuming in your calculations that you will get an order of reinstatement and an additional award. In negotiations with the employer you should assume that you will win the case if it *does* go to a tribunal. Your target is what you would have got had you won the tribunal case, plus an added convenience factor for your kindness in sparing the employer the time, expense and trouble of losing a case before the tribunal.

Even with a well-researched case there is an element of doubt as to which way a tribunal will go. From your side **always take an optimistic view of the outcome!**

Obviously what you can achieve is dependent on the strength of your case, the position of the employer and your negotiating skill. Never forget to stress **the nuisance of a full hearing to the employer**.

A recent study showed that 23 per cent of employers who settled did so because they thought or had been advised that they would lose at a hearing and have to pay more than the agreed sum. About three-quarters of the settlements were £100 or less. Some employers who thought that they might win at a tribunal still saw settlement as a cheaper option. Cost was important. One employer said: 'The settlement cost less than the solicitor's fee to attend the hearing'. Employers who refused to make any settlement did so because they thought they were in the right or had a good case. Others thought that they would create a bad precedent, harm the morale of managers who carried out the sacking, or that settling would mean that they admitted guilt. (Linda Dickens, 'Unfair Dismissal Applications and the Industrial Tribunal System', *Department of Employment Gazette*, March 1979.)

Once again: do not feel that you have any obligation to settle simply because the conciliation office is involved. Obviously, the employer will try to exploit your problems. The study that we have quoted found that 30 per cent of workers accepted settlements because they felt some sort of pressure to do so, for fear of publicity or not getting a reference. One worker pointed out: 'I was looking for another job and publicity may have made it more difficult'. Other forms of pressure quoted were fear of going to 'court', financial hardship, and general strain and anxiety.

Often it is possible for a good representative to get a satisfactory settlement without the case going to a tribunal. Sometimes the reverse is true. A settlement may be agreed by a member without being vetted by a better informed representative. Sometimes a union representative may agree a settlement and later on receive new information which suggests that a tribunal would have awarded considerably more compensation (see page 16 for differences between conciliated settlements and tribunal awards).

Losing the right to take a case

If an employer makes you an offer which you find acceptable then the employer will generally ask you to sign a statement to the effect that in return for the sum of money you will give up your legal right to take the case to an industrial tribunal.

Under employment legislation, however, **these kind of agreements are void and unenforceable**.

■ X is sacked. She applies to a tribunal. Her employer thinks about the matter. He feels that she has a weak case. He calls in X and after some discussion X agrees to accept £200 in return for agreeing not to go to a tribunal. X then meets her union official who points out that, given the facts of the dismissal and the precedents, X would have had an excellent chance of winning the case and that, given her age, salary, service with the company and future job prospects, she would have had an excellent chance of receiving nearly £1,500.

The agreement is void and X can still take the case to a tribunal. If X wins and is awarded more than £200, the £200 will be taken off compensation. However, if she loses she may have costs awarded against her (see Chapter 11). If she withdraws her tribunal application, then a second application will not be allowed.

However, under the general law an employer who has paid a worker money as part of an agreement not to take a case to a tribunal could still sue in the County Court or the High Court, if a tribunal case *is* brought, in order to recover the sum of money even though the agreement itself is not enforceable.

■ Maddison was made redundant. He was given a cheque for £1,600 and a letter which said that the cheque constituted a 'lump sum payment for severance (including redundancy payment) the acceptance of which is final settlement, leaving you with no outstanding claim against the Council.' Maddison applied to a tribunal for unfair dismissal. The EAT found that the tribunal were right to hold that he could still bring a case. The agreement was void. 'What will be prevented (by this rule) are hasty and imprudent agreements and cases of mis-understandings' (*CEI v Maddison* (1976) IRLR 389 EAT).

In some cases, the union may not wish a worker to take a case to a tribunal.

■ In one case, the NIRC held that although a worker had been required by his union to sign a statement saying that he would not take legal proceedings of any kind, this could not stop him from taking a case to an industrial tribunal. The agreement was void. (*Associated Tunnelling Co. Ltd v Wasilewski* (1973) IRLR 346 NIRC).

Involvement of a conciliation officer

If you or a representative acting on your behalf come to the kind of agreement we have been discussing, when a conciliation officer *has taken action*, then the agreement will *not* be void. It will be binding and you will not be entitled to take the case to an industrial tribunal.

The problem here is that the tribunal have held that an officer *has taken action* even where his involvement has been extremely slight.

■ Mrs Whittaker was dismissed and sent two cheques with a letter which said that the cheques were 'full and final settlement of all claims' and if the sum was not acceptable she should return the cheques. She held on to the cheques but applied to a tribunal. A conciliation officer then phoned both parties and asked for certain documents. This was his only involvement. Some time before the hearing she cashed the cheques. The London tribunal held that this amounted to acceptance by her of the settlement and that the officer had taken action by telephoning so that her case could not proceed. 'All the Act speaks of is taking action and action is what the Conciliation officer undoubtedly took' (*Whittaker v British Mail Order Corporation* (1973) IRLR 296).

The same is true even if all the officer does is record a settlement and he or she plays no other part in the settlement:

■ Moore was suspended by his company after his arrest on suspicion of theft. The company called in a conciliation officer to advise them. During a meeting between Moore and the management, it was made clear to him that there was no chance that he would be given his job back. He agreed to accept £300 and resign. Management then called in the conciliation officer who recorded details of the settlement. He took the parties through the contents of the form he had filled in, to make sure that they realised what they had agreed to, and both parties signed the form. The police then dropped charges against Moore and he claimed unfair dismissal. The tribunal decided by a majority that the case could be heard. It was the duty of the officer to ensure that an agreement was reached which was fair to both sides. To simply record the agreement reached with no advice or comment was not *action*. This decision was overruled by the EAT, Court of Appeal and House of Lords, who said the officer has not a duty to promote a *fair* agreement. He has only a duty to promote agreement. If he records a settlement he has taken action to promote a settlement (*Duport Furniture Products Ltd v Moore and ACAS* (1982) IRLR 31 HL).

What these cases mean in practice is that **you lose your protection against contracting out of the law**. All the employer has to do to see that this protection goes out of the window is to see that an officer records the settlement.

We now find that the fact that the officer merely writes down what may be a totally unreasonable settlement is enough to deprive you of your legal rights.

The only requirement on the officer to push for an equitable settlement is where she or he is attempting to secure reinstatement or re-engagement of the worker. When the discussion is about cash, the conciliation officer does not even have to explain the legal position to the worker.

The fact that the officer is *there* magically makes everything all right: 'The involvement of that officer in the settlement can be assumed to negate the existence of any undue pressure on the weaker side and the law therefore allows such settlements to be regarded as binding' (*O'Rourke v Woolworth Co.* (1978) COIT 747/37).

This position will apply to the presence of the officer at *any* stage (*McKay v Bretts Lubricant Co.* (1978) 742/10 COIT). A Scottish tribunal has now held that a *verbal* agreement once the officer has taken action falls within this exception and you lose your protection (*Napier v Pioneer Aggregates UK Ltd* (1982) s/3159/81).

Remember: officers have no responsibility to 'value' a settlement. Their suggestions are aimed at getting an agreement, not a *fair* agreement.

Wording of a settlement

As in all negotiations the exact wording of the final settlement is vital and indeed can prompt another bout of negotiation. A common form of settlement is: 'The employer will pay to the worker the sum of £x in full and final settlement of these proceedings and of all other (if any) claims which the worker may have against the employer.'

You may, however, have several claims. You may have a case of sex or racial discrimination, as well as unfair dismissal. You may have been injured in an accident at work and then sacked for incapability, and be taking a case for compensation as well as unfair dismissal in the civil court before the tribunal. Even phrases like, 'all other claims which the worker could have brought against the employer before an industrial tribunal' will prevent you bringing a whole range of cases.

- The employer will be anxious to avoid all further legal claims and will want the widest possible formulation here.
- You should be precise: 'in full and final settlement of this complaint of unfair dismissal . . . sex discrimination', or whatever your particular action is.

You may become aware of other legal matters later on. You may also want the settlement to go further and state that the dismissal is now accepted by the employer as being unfair or that the employer now agrees that sex discrimination occurred. Obviously, this will help you in the future but may be much more difficult to achieve. Employers will normally be paying you the sum of money in order to *avoid* having such admissions recorded against them. Is this acceptable to you?

You may, however, be able to get an 'open reference' from the employer marked *To Whom It May Concern*, stating your job, periods of employment and satisfactory job performance. Point out this won't cost anything. Make sure your settlement includes a time limit, say 14 days, within which compensation must be paid.

Recording a settlement

If you have come to a final settlement before the hearing, then there are three ways in which the tribunal case can be dealt with:

(1) You simply write a letter to the tribunal withdrawing your application. The tribunal can then dismiss the case. The tribunal has power to award costs where a case is withdrawn but would not do so in these circumstances.

(2) The practice of regional tribunal offices, when they receive a COT3 from the conciliation officer, has been to draw up a decision for the chairman's signature 'that further proceedings in the case are halted except insofar as it is necessary to carry the agreed terms into effect' and then listing the agreed terms in a schedule. The decision is therefore simply to technically adjourn proceedings and may be difficult to enforce against the employer in the County Court.

(3) The worker and employer make a joint application to the Central Office of Tribunals asking that the agreed settlement be approved as a formal tribunal decision to be entered on the public register.

Where a conciliation officer has been involved he or she will fill in the details on form COT3 and, if both sides can agree, this should be forwarded as a joint application to the tribunal. The tribunal will use a standard form of decision recording the acceptance of the terms of settlement.

- The second method has advantages for a worker, as a decision on this basis is not a monetary award within the Employment Protection (Recoupment of Unemployment

Benefit and Supplementary Benefit) Regulations 1977 (see page 219), and the state *cannot* therefore claw back dole or social security benefit that has been paid, as it can with a normal tribunal award.

- The third method has advantages if there is any chance of the employer not meeting his or her obligations under the agreement, as it can be enforced as a normal decision in the County Court.
- If the settlement is going to be useful to the worker getting another job, or in helping with other cases such as disqualification from unemployment benefit, then the fact that the settlement is recorded as a tribunal decision can give it greater legitimacy.

If the employer does not follow the agreement, **then you will have to take an action for breach of contract**. If ACAS has been involved, ring up the ACAS officer if the agreement is not carried out within the time limit, and ask for the employer to be reminded. If this does not work, write to the tribunal explaining what has happened. They may still be able to hear the case but if 'a conciliation officer has taken action' you will have to go for enforcement of your settlement to the County Court or High Court. If you have withdrawn your application you will have to apply again (see page 160).

Summary

(1) Nobody can *stop* you taking a case if you insist, but remember the problem of costs, and in borderline cases be prepared for a preliminary hearing or a re-hearing assessment.

(2) If the employer's IT3 is way out of time, raise it with the tribunal. You may at least get costs and at best a free run.

(3) Are there any circumstances where you might want a preliminary hearing or pre-hearing assessment? If so, ask!

(4) Remember that you may be able to challenge a tribunal decision, if it is based on reasons not previously given by the employer, unless the IT3 has been amended and you were given sufficient time to consider the new grounds.

(5) Generally, there is nothing to be lost by negotiating with the employer over a voluntary settlement. **Make sure that negotiations are based on a well-researched view of the case and the prospect of success at the tribunal.** If you come to an agreement with the employer, you can still take the case to a

tribunal, if you become dissatisfied, *provided* that a conciliation officer was not involved.

(6) In practice it is difficult to avoid a conciliation officer 'taking action'. If the officer is to any degree involved, then any settlement will be binding and you cannot go to a tribunal.

(7) Think carefully before coming to a settlement. Make sure you have completely thought out the position and taken advice before you sign anything.

(8) While going through conciliation, you may receive useful information on the employer's position and attitude to the case – but this can also work against you. You may receive useful advice or information from the conciliation officer – but remember at all times that, as ACAS themselves state: 'Conciliation is by its very nature a negotiating and bargaining process'. **Do not relax your guard simply because the conciliation officer has induced a friendly atmosphere.**

(9) Remember at all times, the conciliation officer is *not* there to guarantee justice or fair play. Be polite and courteous, but firm. **Never rely on the officer.** Do not allow yourself be persuaded by the officer, always adjourn and take advice if a firm offer is made.

(10) Watch the time limits! The fact that you are involved in conciliation does not make it reasonably impracticable for you to present your claim in time. If you are involved in prolonged conciliation and the time limit is running out, you must ask for a postponement (*Ross v NCB* (1974) IRLIB 11/9/74).

(11) Consider carefully the final wording of the statement and the method of disposal.

(12) Ensure that there is constant communication between the union official and worker. Neither should agree to anything without a full discussion with the other. Members should not meet ACAS without their official and vice versa. The union should be involved in all negotiations likely to produce a settlement, though there may have to be exceptions if the member is gullible or too emotionally involved.

7.

Preparing the case

This chapter looks at how to

- dig out the **facts essential** to your case;
- check on an **Act of Parliament relevant** to your case;
- find and use **legal precedents to legitimise** your case; and
- start thinking about **witnesses who can help** your case.

This chapter is written from the point of view of a representative but it should equally help an ordinary worker to prepare a case. It goes into a fair amount of detail, but if you don't have time to prepare your case as fully as this, do as much as you possibly can.

The importance of preparation

A tribunal has to do two things. It has (a) to listen to both sides' conflicting accounts of what actually happened, and (b) to decide what were the facts of the situation. The facts may be established by agreement between the two sides, by direct evidence, or by deduction from other facts. The tribunal then has to look at often different arguments about the law and decide what law applies to these facts. The law may be established by examining the wording of Acts, Regulations and Codes of Practice and the principles established in case law interpreting these legal documents.

You are under a duty to place all the evidence that you think is relevant to your case before the tribunal. It is *not* the tribunal's job to ensure that all relevant evidence is put before it, *even* where one of the parties is *not* legally represented (*Craig v British Railways (Scottish Region)* (1973) 8 ITR 636).

■ It is not in our judgement the duty of any industrial tribunal to enter into the arena and seek to act as the friend of one party or another in deciding the case put before them. That is the basic general rule. We have in this country an adversarial system dealing with these matters and that applies to industrial tribunals as it does to our courts (*Mason v Hamer* (1981) EAT 161/81).

Despite changes in the tribunal regulations giving them more flexibility this is still the basic position.

The same goes for the law. **Don't rely on the tribunal to get the law right.** Put forward interpretation and cases which help your cause and argue as to why they should find on this basis. If you don't, the other side will!

You cannot short-circuit the task of digging out the basic law. Your facts and arguments may be very strong ones from a union viewpoint, but you are not dealing with justice but with the law – which is quite different. Your arguments, however inherently good, need legal justification. You *must* check out the legal sources.

Before you start thinking about how to present your case before a tribunal, **you need to prepare your facts, law and arguments meticulously**. You must know your case inside out down to the smallest details, have thoroughly read the legal points and cases which apply, and have your arguments at your fingertips.

In this sense preparing the basis of a tribunal case is like preparing a negotiating brief. You will know from negotiation that the more homework you have done, the more you are completely familiar with your material, the quicker you can think on your feet if something unexpected happens. The depth and quality of your preparation, if anything, is more important than the manner of presentation.

Someone who has prepared a reasonable case in detail may put it across in a ponderous way, but the strength will emerge. The most brilliant advocate will not get away with lack of preparation; in fact, what looks like brilliant improvisation in negotiation or in court is often actually the product of painstaking research. Again, negotiators will agree that a thorough knowledge of a case instils confidence and improves presentation. Winning the case will be vital to the member so **do not take short cuts**.

Getting the facts

The method used here will be dictated by the circumstances. A representative may have been involved in the case as a negotiator for many months before, say, the worker's dismissal leads to the decision to go to a tribunal. She or he may therefore know all the details intimately. On the other hand, a sudden dismissal may mean that the official is not familiar with the facts, or the member's direct representative may not be able to argue the case before the tribunal.

Many unions issue detailed forms for the member to complete, giving the basic facts in detail. Some will rely on the official initially being given written details by the shop steward. Others simply rely on interviews between the member, the shop steward and the official. **Whatever the circumstances it is important that at an early stage a detailed interview takes place between member and representative(s).**

Where everything is done in writing and the member and the representative meet for half an hour before the case starts is a totally unsatisfactory arrangement. Whichever method you use, you need to know the basic facts below.

Winning the case

 (1) Member's full name and address.
 (2) Employer's full name and address.
 (3) Full address of workplace.
 (4) Date on which member started the employment from which he or she was dismissed.
 (5) Date on which member dismissed.
 (6) Last date on which member worked for employer.
 (7) Member's job description and duties.
 (8) Description of events surrounding dismissal and reasons why you think that the dismissal is unfair.
 (9) Full details of previous warnings, written and verbal.
(10) Name, address and job of others who can support the case.

Bringing home the bacon

 (1) Exact age at time of dismissal.
 (2) Normal hours and total hours worked each week.
 (3) Basic gross pay.
 (4) Average take home pay.
 (5) Income Tax Code No.
 (6) Details of any pension scheme: date of joining; workers' contributions; employer's contribution; options open on termination of employment.
 (7) Details of application for other jobs.
 (8) Details of any new job, name and address of new employer, pay, pension entitlement, date of commencement.

When you meet your member you will either wish to establish these facts for the first time or develop points or omissions in documents she or he has already filled in. **Try to see the member as early as possible** after the incident complained about: *memories can fade*. Distorted recollections can harden. The facts that you are looking for at this stage will be both 'hard' – dates, hours, pay – and 'soft' – the method and manner of dismissal and the reasons for it.

As a general guide to getting the facts, particularly in the soft area, **remember the famous five 'W's which are useful as a mental checklist:**

When did events happen – dates, days, shifts, times?

Where did events happen – the exact places in a particular department, manager's office, machine aisle or canteen?

What exactly did happen – Did A swear *at* B or just swear generally? What precisely was said?

Who was involved besides A and B? Names, jobs, background, attitudes?

Why did things happen as they did? Is the obvious explanation the real explanation?

Remember also the normal guidelines for interviewing:

before the interview work out broadly what kinds of information you need, using the checklists. If relevant, check that the individual *is* a member;

explain the purpose of what you are doing to the member and why you need all this information;

create a relaxed atmosphere. Let the member know that you are on his or her side. She or he may be upset, anxious or worried and may find going back over the details unpleasant. You obviously have to take a different approach with the member who clams up and the member who has verbal diarrhoea;

listen sympathetically and carefully. The first stage is to get your member's version of the facts. At this stage, do not disagree or criticise. Try and leave difficult or distressing questions until the end.

summarise the member's comments at suitable points and ask questions to open up new areas, but otherwise limit your own contribution to when the matter is unclear, unlikely or incredible;

take a record either through notes or a tape recording. Many people will be inhibited if you use a tape; if you take notes, do so when you have got the main shape and detail of the member's story and keep them brief and relevant. Pulling out a notebook at the start or writing down every word may give a feeling of cross-examination and stop the flow of important facts;

go back over the story at the end to ensure that you have got the member's version of what happened right. Particularly, go over at the end any doubtful or contentious areas;

explain the next step and make a concrete arrangement to keep in touch;

do not make promises. At this stage you are still gathering information. Given the limitations in what you know and the vagaries of the law, it is rash to say, 'we're on a winner here';

make a list of documents that the member has and has not got;

make a list of the other people you will need to see to check on the member's story and get a broader picture. Your member may have an emotional or material vested interest in his or her version of the facts but may have left out, misunderstood, distorted or exaggerated important factors. No union official should ever accept anything at face value. You need to check and counter-check, sometimes having to dig deep for the real story. When you have seen the other people involved, see the member again if necessary so that you can discuss and try to reconcile any differences between his or her version and those of other people.

In many legal cases, the representative will take what is called a proof of evidence. This is simply a signed and typed account of the evidence of the member or witness, told in the first person. It may be useful, having checked out the member's story and then cleared up any contradictions. to take a written statement from him or her. This can be used at the tribunal as the basis for your examination of the member or other witnesses. However, at the actual hearing the witnesses will usually have to give oral evidence, not simply read this statement. The only exceptions may be where one side is not represented or a witness has special problems. Knowing that they are going to have to sign their statement can often wonderfully concentrate the mind on the evidence.

Information from the employer

Once you have received the IT3 from the employer (see page 84) you will need to scrutinise it carefully. Representatives need to get their member's reactions. What light does the IT3 shed on the case you are preparing? Are there major conflicts of fact? Do you need to talk to witnesses again? Do you need to ask for further particulars, discovery of documents, or call certain witnesses (see Chapter 8)?

The legal tools

Information on legal rules

Acts of parliament

Check that the facts of your case come within the rules on unfair dismissal, time off, discrimination, etc. laid down by parliament. If you are taking a tribunal case, then you will want to have a look at the Acts of Parliament which apply to tribunal cases (see List of Statutes, page 251).

Legal publishers have recently produced collections of the major Acts of Parliament. These are: *Labour Relations Statutes and Materials* (and Companion Volume 1980–81) and *Employment Law Handbook* (see page 249 for details). These are simply the acts under one cover. There is no commentary.

Reading an act

Acts are written in legal mumbo jumbo. To get the facts you want you may have to jump from section to section and sometimes from act to act. It is best to look at the act in conjunction with a legal guide which gives you the substance of the law and the relevant sections of the act. The only way to learn how to read an act effectively is through experience.

At the front you will find a contents list or index headed 'Arrangement of Sections'. If you do not know the section you want, look here first.

You will find that an act consists of parts where it covers a number of areas, grouping those areas into similiar topics; sections which spell out the substance of the law; and schedules which you will find at the back of the act and which give you more detailed technical information on particular sections and list details of amendments to earlier legislation including which parts of it have been repealed.

The sections which are the bones of the act will be grouped together under cross-headings. This makes it easier for you to find the relevant group of sections as you glance through. For example, in the EP(C)A there are six sections under the cross-heading 'time off work', seven under the cross-heading 'guarantee payments', both grouped together with 'suspension from work on medical grounds' in Part II of the act, 'rights arising in the course of employment'.

Next to each section you will find marginal notes which will help you to identify the gist of that particular section.

Each section is divided into subsections and sub-subsections. For example, if you had been refused permission to attend a shop stewards' training course and you wished to cite the law to the tribunal, you would be bringing a complaint under 2.27 (1)(b).

You have to read an act slowly asking what the precise meaning of each word is. There are many key words and phrases which have a precise legal meaning as you can see from this book. The right to time off, which s.27 of the EP(C)A gives union officials, is limited to 'working hours'. If you look further at s.32 you will find a definition of what is meant by 'working hours'.

In most acts you will find an interpretation section, generally under the cross-heading 'miscellaneous and supplementary'. For example, under s.27 of the EP(C)A it is only officials of recognised independent trade unions who are eligible for the time-off rights. You would find a definition of independent trade union in the interpretation section, s.153 of the act.

For a definition of 'recognised' you would have to turn to s.32(1)(a), which says 'a trade union shall be treated as recognised not only if it is recognised for the purposes of collective bargaining but also if the ACAS . . .'

But you can go further: if you look at s.32(2) you will see: 'In subsection (1) – "collective bargaining" means negotiations related to or connected with one or more of the matters specified in section 29(1) of TULRA 1974 . . .' So you would have to go back to TULRA to find out exactly what the situation was.

The same would be true if you wanted to know exactly what the term 'official' in s.27 means. You would find this definition nowhere in the EP(C)A but in s.30 of TULRA.

You may also find certain definitions in the schedules to an act. For example, schedule 14 of the EP(C)A lays down guidelines on how to calculate 'normal working hours' and a week's pay.

For greater guidance on what a particular section means, you need to go first to any relevant Code of Practice and then to any relevant case law.

Whether you get the facts you want regarding an Act of Parliament from the act itself, or a guide to legislation, **these are some points that you ought to check to establish that you have a full understanding**.

- **Are any groups of workers not covered?** We have looked at this earlier.
- **Are there any qualifying conditions?** Must you have worked 52 weeks or two years? Must you be an official of an independent recognised trade union?
- **Are there any employers' defences?** e.g. The employer does not have to give a woman returning from maternity leave her previous job back if he or she can show it was 'not reasonably practicable'.
- **What is the basic right the sections establish?** A right to time off for whom? When? For what purposes? On what conditions?
- **Are there key words or phrases requiring interpretation?** In other sections of the act, the interpretation section, the schedules? In a Code of Practice? In cases?
- **How do you enforce the right?** For the rights we are talking about here, through tribunals?
- **Is there a time limit?** We have seen the problems here.
- **What do you get out of it?** Compensation? Recommendations?

Codes of Practice

Great Britain	Six Counties
ACAS Code of Practice 1	*LRA Code of Practice 1*
Disciplinary Practice and Procedure in Employment	*Disclosure of Information*
ACAS Code of Practice 2	*LRA Code of Practice 2*
Disclosure of Information to Trade Unions for Collective Bargaining Procedures	*Disciplinary Practice and Procedure in Employment*
ACAS Code of Practice 3	*LRA Code of Practice 3*
Time off for Trade Union Duties and Activities	*Time off for Trade Union Duties and Activities*
Code of Practice on Picketing	
Code of Practice on Closed Shop	

Each Code costs 15p except *Picketing* and *The Closed Shop* which are free. The *Industrial Relations Code* costs 30p, again from HMSO.

Government guides

Simple guides on the whole range of tribunal law are published by the Department of Employment in the United Kingdom and the Department of Manpower Services and N. Ireland Training Executive in the Six Counties. These guides are free.

- Some are good and detailed such as those on the redundancy payments and contracts of employment legislation, others are skimpier.
- They are often useful for a quick check up on the law but if you are taking a case it is sensible to go to the act itself.
- Make sure you have an up-to-date version of the particular guide.

Other guides are mentioned in Further Reading at the end of this book.

Information on case law

Cases are vital weapons to use before a tribunal. Having assembled your facts, you will be on the look-out for cases decided on similar facts. There are three periodicals which may be useful here:

(1) *Bargaining Report* is published by the Labour Research Department six times a year. It costs £6.42 a year (£4.92 if your union is affiliated to the LRD).

(2) *Incomes Data Brief.* This is published by a commercial company twice monthly and contains brief articles on labour law developments and case reports relevant to trade unions and management (£40 per annum). Periodically Incomes Data publish supplements to their briefs which subscribers receive and which are booklets listing the basic case law on particular topics, such as unfair dismissal compensation, time off, or discrimination at work.

(3) *Industrial Relations Review and Report Legal Information Bulletin* is also published by a commercial company; this fulfils a similar function to the *Incomes Data Brief.* It is much dearer at £60 per annum.

Your district or divisional office should have access to at least one of these series. (For further reading, see pages 249–50.) From time to time they will have articles summarising the case law on a particular topic, such as dismissal for theft, or indirect discrimination, or time off for safety representatives, as well as having regular reports on the latest cases over the whole area of tribunal law. All of these publications, and some of the books you will find listed under 'Further Reading', can give you a lead. By scanning through them you may find cases relevant to your problem. However, you will only find a brief précis of the facts and decisions.

Law reports

If you have located a case you wish to use, the next stage is to read a full report of the decision. The problem with citing the brief report in *Incomes Data Brief* is that it may miss out a statement particularly useful to your case, or miss out qualifications or modifications in its short statement of the case. Often a general statement of the law by the tribunal chairperson or judge will be most useful; you will be able to quote it at the hearing. You have to go to the horse's mouth.

There are a series of law reports which give the full detailed judgements and these are what you will want to cite at the hearing.

- **IRLR** *Industrial Relations Law Reports:* these are published monthly by Industrial Relations Law Reports and concentrate on cases which will be of practical use to trade unions and management.
- **ICR** *Industrial Case Reports:* these are again a specialist series, produced by the 'official' Incorporated Council of Law Reporting. They are published monthly and in a single annual volume.
- **QB** *Queens Bench Division Reports:* published by the ICLR in volumes each year, cover all cases, not just labour law.
- **WLR** *Weekly Law Reports:* published by the ICLR in weekly parts and then in three annual volumes. They cover all the reports that will later appear in the official series as well as cases which will not appear elsewhere. Again, they are *general*, not just covering labour law.
- **All ER** *All England Law Reports:* also cover all kinds of legal cases and are published weekly by Butterworths Ltd, and then in three annual parts.

There are also two series of reports which have now stopped publication but which may help you if you are looking up older cases:

- **KIR** *Knights Industrial Reports* – 1967–1975.
- **ITR** *Industrial Tribunal Reports* – 1965–1978.

A union district or divisional office which deals with tribunal cases should have access to one of the specialist series ICR or IRLR. Otherwise you will be dependent on libraries. The central public library in cities will generally have one of these series as well as a selection of the more general series. Another avenue will be the library in a university, or polytechnic or college.

Cases are cited by lawyers in a certain way. *White v University of Manchester* (1976) IRLR 218 EAT means that White was taking legal action against Manchester University, and that, having lost at the tribunal, she appealed to EAT. You will find the report of the case in the 1976 run of *Industrial Relations Law Reports* on page 218. Where reports are produced weekly or monthly, the pages are numbered consecutively over the year. At the end of the citation is the name of the court. This is imortant, given the system of precedent.

You will be on the lookout for EAT and CA cases and more modern cases. But don't neglect IT cases. They are persuasive and should be given strong consideration by a tribunal where there is no higher authority.

Remember: if a case is crucial, check to see if it is reported. If it is not then do not be afraid to cite it even though you have simply read a short report in the *Incomes Data Brief* or the *Industrial Relations Legal Information Bulletin*. If it is not reported you will see a reference after it, e.g. *Pearson v Tameside MB* (1978) COIT 785/191 (a tribunal case), or *Smith v Stanley Davidson* (1978) EAT 44/78 (an appeal case). If you cite it this way, the tribunals will be able to get copies from the central office or EAT. The case will be just as much an authority even though it is not reported. Cases you read about like this may of course be reported later, so don't give up too easily.

Witnesses

In a recent tribunal case, a worker was dismissed for being absent without permission. The management asserted that no permission had been granted to the worker, and that time could only be taken off after discussion with the shop steward and foreman. Neither the steward nor the foreman were present to give evidence. This often happens.

Trade unionists do not use witnesses sufficiently in tribunal cases. A tribunal will listen to evidence such as: 'The shop steward, Jill Jones, said that the warning was not acceptable to the union and should be scrubbed from the record'. They will place far more weight on it if Jill Jones is there and says it herself. Sworn verbal evidence which is subject to cross-examination is going to help you sway the tribunal much more than hearsay evidence (see page 183) or written submissions.

There is often a direct conflict of evidence where neither side has called witnesses who could clear the matter up. Faced with contradictory assertions the tribunal have to decide which side's story they find most credible.

If a witness can give evidence which is relevant and helpful to the case, you should strongly consider calling her or him to establish facts about the incident you are complaining about, the member's past record, the member's character, general relationships at the workplace, or the company's policy and industrial relations practices.

If you decide someone *can* give helpful evidence, the next question is *will* they? For example, do they suffer from verbal diarrhoea, will they listen to questions and not simply confuse the issue? On the other hand, are they so reticent as to make a negligible impression? An irrelevant or unhelpful witness can actually set your case back. Can the witness's evidence not only help the member but also damage him or her? For example, whilst the witness knows that on this particular day the member did not spend the afternoon at a nearby pub instead of work, is cross-examination likely to reveal that this *had* happened on two other days in that particular week?

How is the witness's bearing likely to affect the tribunal? There are many honest and sincere witnesses who come across as evasive and shifty simply because of their uneasiness in a foreign climate. This is unfortunate, but in the end it is the impression on the tribunal that counts. The EAT in *Paterson v Barratt Developments (Aberdeen) Ltd* (1977) IRLR 214 stated that a tribunal can take demeanour into account when assessing the credibility of a witness. **You should:**

(1) **Decide whether you want to call a person as a witness**, remembering that the other side will have the right to cross-examine and that the most damaging witness is one who gives evidence adverse to your side. *Do not* play the numbers game and call a lot of witnesses because you think it looks good. All witnesses can be cross-examined and this may bring out matters that will *not* help your case.

(2) **Interview the witness** and take a written record of evidence.

(3) Before the case **take the witness through the evidence** and explain the *type* of questions you will ask on the stand but do not rehearse a word-for-word recital, because this will look highly artificial and perhaps even break down.

(4) **Explain** to the witness the *kind* of questions the tribunal will be likely to ask in the context of his or her evidence.

(5) **Give the witness examples** of the *kind* of challenging cross-examination to expect from the employer's representatives. Pick on the weak points of his or her evidence to see how it stands up. Again, do not rehearse precise questions.

(6) It may be useful for a **witness to observe another tribunal case** to see how the procedure operates.

(7) **Point out to the witness** that the main thing is to remain calm, and politely, slowly and specifically to answer questions on the basis of the evidence.

(For more on witnesses see pages 143 and 166).

Putting it all together

Example (a):

Joan Smith, a shift worker, is elected convenor. This is a full-time post. The previous, long-standing convenor had worked days before his election and had been paid at a day rate. Smith argues that she should be paid shift rate – the difference is about £10 a week. The company say that the matter is covered by the agreement for a phased reduction of earnings for those workers switching from shifts to days.

Negotiations centre around basic arguments:

- You, the relevant union officer and Smith argue that the company agree that one steward should be full-time, and she is the democratic choice. Why should she lose money for doing the union job?
- The management argue that Smith will not be subject to the inconvenience and problems of shifts. Why should she receive shift rate? She is now on days.
- The management argue that Smith's situation is clearly covered by the transfer agreement.
- You argue that this covers transfer for 'medical or operational reasons'. Smith's transfer is not covered.

You basically argue that it is a small and paltry concession for management to make, but there are no precedents and you get nowhere. You decide to take the case to a tribunal.

Step 1: You make a note of the basic facts and arguments and establish that Smith is qualified.

Step 2: You look up the EP(C)A s.27. You see that s.27(2) states that if a steward is allowed time off for union duties and is a time worker she or he should be paid *'as if he had worked at that work for the whole of that time'*. You puzzle over this. Does 'that work' refer to nights or days? You find difficulty in getting much more help from the section.

Step 3: You look at the Code of Practice on *Time Off*. All you can find is a rather vague statement that unions may face problems which 'may arise for example from the differing hours or shifts worked by members in a single negotiating area'. Not very helpful.

Step 4: You go to the IRLR/ten year index under 800: 'Employment Protection Rights'. You see 850: 'Time off for Trade Union Duties'. There are no further sub-headings. The first three cases listed when you dig them out do not seem in point. But no. 4 is *McCormick v Shell Chemicals* (1979) IRLR 40. Its facts are very close to your case . . . and the union got a result.

In this case, the tribunal studied s.27(3) and appear to have interpreted 'that work' to mean the shift work the steward in the case had previously done, so that he should be paid at shift rate for the time he spent on union duties.

They then looked at s.27(5) which says that a steward's right to be paid under the act whilst carrying out his duties should not affect his right to be paid under his contract of employment. The tribunal found that, as he was entitled to be paid shift rate under his contract, he was still entitled to be paid that rate when he took time off for union activities. They also felt that these kind of cases should be looked at in terms of the act's intention that workers should not lose money whilst on trade-union duties.

Step 5: This case is a tribunal decision. With a relatively recent right like time off, it takes some years before you get higher authority on many points. This case should help, but you check through the other cases just to see if there is an EAT decision which will polish off the employer without a scintilla of a doubt. There isn't, but *McCormick v Shell* should strengthen your case (remember precedents from other tribunals are *persuasive* not *binding*, see page 13).

Example (b):
There is a night shift and a day shift at Crawfords Cardboard Boxes Ltd. There are nine night shift stewards and 16 day shift stewards. From time to time the night shift stewards are required to attend a meeting with the day shift stewards to discuss general matters. The custom and practice has been for management to pay the night shift stewards three hours at night rates. They now inform the union that in future the three hours' pay will not include night premium. Negotiations break down and a decision is made to take the case to a tribunal.

Step 1: The facts of this case are clearly different from *McCormick v Shell*, but you cannot find a reported case with similar facts. Look again at McCormick's case: the facts are different but the principle is similar. If the night stewards had worked *at that work* for the whole of the three hours they were allowed for meeting the day stewards, they would have been working at night shift rates. You would, therefore, be able to use McCormick.

Step 2: However, you then need to look at the differences between the two cases to find your weak points. You should also work out what the employer is likely to argue, like:

- In the McCormick case, the shop steward would have lost money. His case must be seen in the context of the policy of the act that stewards should not lose by doing union work. In example (b) the stewards would not *directly* lose.
- Under their contracts of employment the stewards at Crawfords were *not* entitled to be paid three extra hours at night rate.

Step 3: You could then reply that the stewards *were* contractually entitled to be paid night rate while working, and were *still* entitled to be paid that rate when on union activities, and that *that* was the legal point made in McCormick. The stewards here would lose by not being paid their contractual rate for extra work – in fact they should be paid overtime.

Even if the facts are different, look closely at the case, but anticipate arguments on the differences.

Example (c):
Tom Herman, a shop steward, was very friendly with the manager, Gene Larford. He refused to take up a grievance for one of

his members who called him a 'management man'. A fight broke out and the member was hospitalised. Both claimed that the other started it. After a full inquiry, according to procedure, management sacked Tom and the member. The member has found a better job but Tom wants to claim unfair dismissal at a tribunal, arguing that there is nothing in the works' rules that prohibits fighting.

You know that misconduct is potentially a fair reason for dismissal and that management can dismiss for one incident where there is proven gross misconduct.

On looking up the cases you would come across *Parsons & Co. Ltd v McLoughlin* (1978) IRLR 65 EAT. On reading this case you would find that there was little point in taking Tom's case further. This is an EAT decision and the facts are the same.

You would see that the EAT accept that fighting is generally gross misconduct which can involve danger at work and the risk of serious injury to others, and dealt with the main argument that there was nothing in McLoughlin's contract that forbade fighting by saying: 'It ought not to be necessary for anybody let alone a shop steward to have in black and white in the form of a rule that a fight is something which is going to be regarded very gravely by management'. End of the road for Tom.

Example (d):

Mike O'Neil, member of the TGWU branch committee and a safety representative at Greenfield Chemicals, was acting shop steward for two months, December 1982 – January 1983, whilst the regular steward was ill. On 18 January 1983, it was agreed that the convenor and certain stewards should visit sick employees who had been sent letters indicating that they might be sacked in the near future. The following day the convenor asked Mike to accompany him on one of the visits. The superintendent refused him permission. He went anyway and was absent for one and a half hours. On the following Monday, management attempted to issue Mike with a written warning. The convenor argued that according to the Code of Practice a steward should not be disciplined prior to full discussions with a senior rep or full-time official.

No warning was ever given though one and a half hours' money was docked.

On Thursday 15 February and Friday 16 February 1983, there was a combined committee meeting at Mike's site involving

TGWU and AUEW. The normal practice was that TGWU stewards from the host site attended as of right whilst branch committee members attended 'subject to work requirements'. On Tuesday 13 February Mike informed his foreman that he would attend the meeting. This was the normal procedure.

On the Thursday, Mike attended the meeting. On Friday, as he was making a report to the meeting, the phone rang. It was the superintendent who told him rudely to come back to work as he felt that T&G representation at the meeting was already adequate. Mike reported this to the meeting. They said he should stay as they felt this was an attempt to prevent him attending the meeting rather than a genuine work requirement. The convenor then phoned the works manager and explained that Mike's presence was important to the meeting, as he was in fact making a report, but the manager again confirmed that Mike should return to work, this time stating that the reason was work requirements. The committee agreed that he should stay. He was suspended and dismissed.

Step 1: Pick out the salient facts:

- safety rep branch committee member former acting steward;
- January incident – misconduct but industrial relations business. No warning actually given;
- February incident: committee men attended 'subject to work requirements'. Asked permission according to normal procedure. Management attempted to withdraw in middle of meeting, giving two different reasons. Rudeness. Committee agreed that he should stay.

Step 2: Pursue the salient facts:

- interview the convenor;
- interview others who attended the meeting, preferably from other sites;
- interview the foreman;
- do management agree with this version?
- any past examples of this kind of incident. What were the decisions here?
- what exactly were the work requirements management argued? Did they exist and were they justified?
- does the background leave the story untouched? How long has Mike worked there? Has he otherwise a clear record?

Were management gunning for him for other reasons such as his union activities?

Step 3: Pick out the basic arguments:

- if we do accept the January incident as misconduct, he was on union business accompanied by the convenor, not on a personal jaunt. The absence was short;
- money had been docked but no written warning was on record concerning this incident. Nor would the union have been prepared to accept such a warning, on the grounds that such a severe penalty was inappropriate to the circumstances;
- in February his record was therefore clear. He had received permission to attend the meeting as far as he and the union were concerned. This was supported by the fact that his absence on Thursday was not challenged;
- management should be able to minimally plan ahead. Had they informed the union *before* the meeting of the situation as to work requirements the position would have been different;
- the first telephone call gave the reason for recall as adequate TGWU representation, an invalid reason. The committee therefore saw the second work requirements reason as a hastily contrived excuse. Moreover, management were rude and abrupt. The decision that he should remain was that of the committee;
- management did not point out to Mike the consequences to him of refusing to return to work;
- given these points, dismissal was far too harsh a penalty and unreasonable in all the circumstances.

Step 4: Pick out likely management arguments. (At first you will have to do this on the basis of the information you have. Later the IT3 and further particulars and discovery may help.)

- will they be able to produce witnesses to deny any of the points in your evidence, for example, that the first telephone call argued 'adequate representation'?
- the fact that the January warning was not given was a technicality. All agreed blatant misconduct *had* occurred, in that permission for absence was specifically refused;
- management interpreted the work requirement exception to mean that representatives could be withdrawn *during*

extended meetings. This allowed representatives some participation in meetings;

- a work situation had occurred on the Friday that they had not seen on the Thursday, which required Mike's recall;
- there was no need to warn him of the consequences of his disobedience. The committee were all experienced trade unionists, and should have advised him to return to work. The matter could then have been negotiated to avoid future similar problems.

What relationship do these arguments bear to the facts? How can they be answered? What witnesses are management likely to call?

Step 5: Pick out relevant parts of the Codes of Practice on *Discipline* and *Time Off*:

- you can argue that the whole intention of the code puts the obligation on management to organise time off in advance: 'Where it is necessary for the union to hold meetings . . . during working hours it should seek to agree the arrangements with management as far in advance as practicable . . . Management may want time off to be deferred . . . the grounds for postponement should be made clear . . . (paras 26 and 28);
- you can argue that knowing requirements in advance, management should make arrangements for cover. Management is responsible for making 'the operational arrangements for time off . . . Management and the unions should seek to agree arrangements where necessary for other employees to cover the work of officials or members taking time off' (para 25).

Step 6: Pick out any case which can justify and legitimise your arguments and weaken management's:

- if you look up the IRLR index you will find: 234.17 'Unauthorised leaving of job site'; 234.36 'Refusal to obey an order'; and 234.37 'Insubordination';
- this should put you on the track of cases such as *Rasool and another v Hepworth Pipe Co. Ltd No. 2* (1980) IRLR 137 EAT; *UCATT v Brain* (1981) IRLR 224 CA down to *Talbot v Hugh M. Fulton* (1975) IRLR 52 and *Greenslade v Hoveringham Gravels Ltd* (1975) IRLR 114. Whilst the

facts of these cases are different from those here, they make the point that a worker's refusal to obey an order must be wilful or deliberate, made in the knowledge that his behaviour could result in dismissal, and that it may be unfair to dismiss where it was unreasonable to issue the order in the first place.

You can argue that these principles apply to the confused circumstances in the meeting here;

- you should also be able to dig out from these references cases such as *Pringle v Lucas Industrial Equipment Ltd* (1975) IRLR 266 and *Lindsey v Fife Forge Co. Ltd* (1976) IRLR 47, which held that statements in written procedures which do not specify that absence will lead to summary dismissal but use such phrases as 'will tender themselves liable to' or 'may be subject to' do not automatically justify summary dismissal;

- when you look up the index on 'time off' and dig out the cases, you will find no case in point. However, you may come across an *Incomes Data Brief* supplement which lists many unreported cases. Here you will find two cases: *Pearson v Tameside MB* (1978) COIT 785/191 – branch secretary unfairly dismissed for taking four days off without the permission of management to catch up on backlog of union duties; and *Smith v Stanley Davidson* (1978) EAT 44/78 – steward held to be unfairly dismissed for attending a union course against his employer's wishes. These cases should help, *but note* that in both there was contribution, i.e. the representative was held partly to blame and his compensation was reduced. You will, therefore, need to argue against that in this case.

Step 7: Make a list of documents and witnesses: in this case you will want to make use of several witnesses, for example, the convenor, other members of the committee and, *crucially*, the foreman who was informed of the meeting.

Step 8: You will want to put together your facts, arguments and law in the context of the actual hearing. Look at the strengths of your case to emphasise them. Look at the weaknesses to reinforce them:

- *always* eliminate the surplus or irrelevant facts;
- *always* discard arguments which appear superficially attractive, but which may lead to problems;

● a tribunal is unlikely to want to know details of Mike O'Neil's life story *before* the relevant incidents if his disciplinary record is clean. That's all you need to mention. They are not likely to want to know full details of the sick members he visited in the January incident.

In the same way, you may at first be attracted to an argument that Mike was victimised because of his trade-union membership and activities. Taking this further, you would find that the tribunals have interpreted this phrase in a narrow and technical manner and, secondly, that there is not much evidence showing that this was the management's intention. If you raise this at the hearing, it may be time consuming and obscure the real issues. You have a good case on general unfair dismissal principles so *do not* put your eggs in the trade-union activities basket.

8.

Building the case

As you start preparing your or your member's case in the way outlined in the last chapter, you may find that you require facts and documents which you can only get from the employer. This chapter gives you details of some of the ways you can:

- obtain further details of your opponent's case;
- obtain documents important to the preparation of your case; and
- ensure important witnesses will attend the hearing.

Where to find the law
Industrial Tribunals Regulations 4
EP(C)A sch. 91(7)
Sex Discrimination Act s.74
Race Relations Act s.65

Building the case

Certain procedures are laid down by the regulations to help either side build up their case. Often these procedures are not used, but sometimes you will need to use them to develop an effective case. As Sir John Donaldson once said:

> Cases are intended to be heard with all the cards face upwards on the table. The tribunal's powers of ordering further and better particulars, discovery or issuing witness orders will be of little value in the pursuit of justice if the parties do not know they exist. Tribunals should therefore be vigilant to ensure that their existence is known in appropriate cases (*Copson v Eversure Accessories* (1974) ICR 636 NIRC).

Most of the matters between application and hearing – known as interlocutory matters – are dealt with by a chairperson alone.

Further and better particulars

We have seen that within certain rules neither side is limited to what they have said on the IT1 and the IT3. At the hearing you can raise new issues and ask for further information. However, this may mean that you are not fully prepared to deal with new arguments or information, or that you will have to ask for an adjournment which can lead to long delays and perhaps further expense. It is generally better to know as precisely as possible what you are up against before the hearing, so that you can prepare your arguments and evidence in detail.

You are, therefore, entitled to ask for further details before the hearing to help you in preparing your case.

The employer is asked to give details of his reasons for dismissal and sufficient particulars of the grounds on which he is going to resist the case on the IT3. If you feel that the employer's statements are too vague, brief or unintelligible, then you are entitled to ask for more information.

Some employers have been known to simply state on the IT3, 'The reason for dismissal is one which will be found justifiable if the case is heard by a tribunal'. You should also check the reasons given by the employer on the IT3 with any written statement given to the workers of the reasons for dismissal. If the reason is different, you may need more details.

For example: if all you can glean from an IT3 in terms of reasons, grounds and particulars is: 'Joan Smith was sacked for swearing', then you will want to know more. You would want to know:

(1) What words were allegedly used?
(2) When and where did the alleged incidents take place?
(3) Were there any witnesses?

If all you can extract from the IT3 is: 'The applicant was warned on several occasions about incompetent workmanship', then you will want to know:

(1) What were the examples of incompetent work; what should the worker have done, and how did she or he fall short?
(2) How many warnings were given?
(3) Were they verbal or written?
(4) When were the warnings given, and what stage of the disciplinary procedure did they represent?

The purpose of further particulars is to find out *exactly* what the employer is saying, not to give you the detailed evidence that will be used to back up his or her allegations. In the first example above, questions such as whether swearing was common in the worker's job, or whether the person she swore at had sworn at her, would be matters of evidence. Obviously, the line is a fine one and ultimately it is up to the tribunal to decide what you can get away with. The regulations do say that the tribunal has the power to tell the employer to furnish further particulars of the grounds on which he or she relies and of any facts and contentions relevant thereto – an expression which could even cover legal arguments.

Remember: the tribunal itself can ask either side for more details and tribunal chairpersons will scrutinise forms to ensure that they meet the rules. Tribunals have a discretion as to whether or not they make an order but they should be sympathetic to requests from either side for further particulars, as it is in their interest to narrow the area of dispute and get onto the table exactly what the dispute is about.

However, in the past tribunals have sometimes been reluctant to grant further particulars on the grounds that it will make tribunal cases more formal and complex. The attitude in earlier cases was summed up by Mr Justice Phillips: 'To introduce a formal system of discovery and inspection . . . might in the abstract produce more perfect justice but it would be at such great costs in time, money and manpower that the whole machinery would grind to a halt.' (*Stone v Charrington* (1977) 12 ITR 255 EAT.) However, this attitude changed:

■ White was sacked by Manchester University. The IT3 stated she was dismissed because she was: (a) unable to cope with the duties associated with her job; and (b) her attitude to students and other employees caused ill feeling and difficulty which confirmed the view she was unsuitable. She sought further particulars of: (a) the respects in which she was unable to cope; and (b) the ways in which her attitude was said to be defective. Her appeal against a decision not to grant her the further details was upheld. She would not know the case against her in sufficient detail to prepare an answer and inevitably she would have to apply for an adjournment at the hearing. 'We do not wish to say anything to encourage unnecessary legalism to creep into the proceedings but while that should be avoided, it should not be avoided at the expense of falling into a different error, that of doing injustice by a hearing taking place when the party who has to meet the allegations does not know what those allegations are' (*White v University of Manchester* (1976) IRLR 218 EAT).

Requesting further particulars

Step 1: Write to the employer. There is an example of a letter to an employer requesting further particulars on page 134:

- be as specific as possible;
- write as soon as possible after you receive the IT3, to give you more time to prepare your case;
- always put in a short time limit;
- send a copy to the tribunal;
- use recorded delivery.

Step 2: If you receive no reply inside the time limit, or the reply does not meet the requirements laid down in your letter, wait a day or two. Then write to the tribunal asking for an order to be made that the employer produce the further particulars within a short time limit, say seven days. Send a copy to the employer.

Step 3: The application is dealt with by a chairperson sitting alone. The order will usually be made without hearing the other side, but the party against whom the order is made may apply to have it varied or set aside. A party who is served with an order to provide particulars within a certain time can ask for an extension of that time.

Step 4: If it is granted, the order will be sent to the employers or their representative. It will normally have a time limit by which the particulars should be supplied to you. You will receive a copy to keep you in the picture.

Step 5: If a party *is* ordered to provide further particulars and does not do so, then the tribunal may strike out the case and an employer may be barred from defending.

The use of this power is in the tribunal's discretion. They will take into account a number of factors in deciding whether a person should be disqualified, including whether or not she or he is represented and whether or not the tribunal has explained what is required by an order of further particulars and the possible consequences of not obeying it.

General Workers Union

31 Westward Road

Brownpool

Dear Sir/Madam,

CLAIM FOR UNFAIR DISMISSAL - JOAN SMITH - CASE NUMBER:

I represent Joan Smith in her claim for unfair dismissal. The
Notice of Appearance entered by your company does not provide
sufficient particulars for me to be able to prepare my member's
case. I would be obliged therefore if you would supply the
following particulars under question 5 of the IT 3 form:

1. Please state exactly the nature of the misconduct. Please
   itemise each incident or omission complained of and specify
   when and where each occurred.

2. Is it alleged that the applicant has been guilty of misconduct
   in the past? If so, please give particulars of each occasion
   relied upon and specify whether it is alleged that the applicant
   was given any warning in respect of the acts complained of.

3. If it is to be alleged that the applicant was given warnings
   in respect of the acts complained of, please state precisely:

   a) when each and every warning relied upon was given;

   b) where such warnings were given;

   c) by whom such warnings were given;

   d) the actual words used;

   e) whether such warnings were verbal or in writing and if
      in writing please produce the relevant documents;

   f) whether such warnings were in accordance with any disciplinary
      code or prodedure, and if so please produce that code or
      procedure.

4. Please produce the company works rules relied upon.

We feel these details to be essential to our case and a full and
speedy hearing. Please provide the above particulars within the
next 10 days.

Yours faithfully

A. O'Fishall

cc: Secretary of the Industrial Tribunals

Sample letter: request for orders for further particulars

■ Morritt, an unrepresented applicant, was ordered to provide further particulars. He asked for more time to provide these, then he wrote to ask the employers what information they wanted. They said they 'wanted to know the grounds of his claim for unfair dismissal'. He wrote back: 'I allege that I have been dismissed through victimisation and that dishonesty has been used to gain my dismissal'. At the hearing the tribunal dismissed the case as Morritt had not complied with the order. The EAT said this was wrong. He did not understand what he had to do and the tribunal had not explained to him that he might have his case dismissed at the hearing (*Morritt v London Borough of Lambeth* (1979) EAT 244).

■ Martin took an unfair dismissal case against his employers. His IT1 stated that 'the procedure was unfair' and that the 'respondent did not act reasonably'. An order for further particulars was made and Martin's solicitor was told that if they were not provided the case would be dismissed. No further particulars were provided and the case was struck out. The EAT upheld this decision (*Martin v London Transport Executive* (1979) EAT 400).

The tribunal must send notice to a party in default before disqualification, giving them an opportunity to explain why this should not be done.

■ The aim of disqualification is to protect the other side, not to punish the defaulter, so when an order was made in respect of discrimination allegations and not complied with, the tribunal were wrong to dismiss the case completely, when unfair dismissal was also being claimed. The case should have been heard on that head (*Dean v Islamic Foundation* (1982) IRLR 290 CA).

Remember: If *you* do not give sufficient detail on your application form the employer can get an order requesting further particulars against *you*!

■ Whitley was sacked for submitting a fraudulent expenses claim. He took an unfair dismissal case claiming that other workers had been involved in the same practice over a long period and that this fiddling was condoned by the company. They asked for further particulars and the regional chairperson turned them down. This decision was overruled. The company were entitled to know precisely what the case against them was, so that they could prepare their own evidence. Whitley was trying to say that the employers' reason for dismissal was not a good reason because of special circumstances and the employer was entitled to know what these circumstances were (*ICL v Whitley* (1978) IRLR 318 EAT).

The 1980 Tribunal regulations bend over backwards to help the bosses. Under the old rules employers could ask for further particulars only *after* they had entered a Notice of Appearance (see page 86). The new rules give the gaffers the right to ask for further particulars *before* they put in a defence. Whether their request is granted will be up to the tribunal.

You have to **remember your employer's right to request further particulars** when you are filling in your IT1.

■ Colonial Mutual Life Assurance received a copy of an IT1 from Clinch. He was claiming unfair dismissal. The company applied for further particulars of all the facts he would put before the tribunal if they came to assess compensation. The EAT turned this request down. It would set a precedent which would make cases far too technical. However, under para 13 when asked to state what in his opinion was the reason for his sacking, he had stated 'redundancy/victimisation'. The EAT held that even though the onus of proof was on the employers they were entitled to further particulars (*Colonial Mutual Life Assurance Society Ltd v Clinch* (1981) ICR 752 EAT).

Employers may increasingly use this weapon. **So be prepared!**

Discovery of documents

We have discussed the kind of documentary back-up that you will need to justify and strengthen your case (see checklist on page 82). If you have not got some of the documents listed which may be relevant to your case, then you should write to the employer as soon as possible requesting copies. The employer is more likely to have these documents than you are. The kind of letter you might send is illustrated on page 138. Send it recorded delivery and always keep copies. Once again, if the employer refuses to send you the required documents, you can apply to the tribunal who can order him or her to do so (letter on page 139).

This procedure can lead to delays and prolong the case. **If you**

need documentation, start the ball rolling as early as possible.

With most cases such as unfair dismissal, discovery should be fairly straightforward. The documents you want will be relatively non-contentious.

- In a claim that an employer has failed to inform a union of redundancy 'at the earliest opportunity', you may want details of forward planning, purchase of new machinery, sales figures, management memos, which reflect on the employer's argument that the union was notified as early as possible.

  ■ Taylor was sacked by his boss Ms Waters. He claimed that he was unfairly dismissed. 'No you were not', she answered, 'you were made redundant because there was not enough work for you.' Taylor therefore applied to the tribunal for discovery of company records, orders, invoices and receipts relating to the work he had been doing so that he could establish whether there had been a fall off. The tribunal granted discovery. He was entitled to see whether there had been a diminution of work sufficient to make him redundant. The EAT upheld this decision. To prepare his case properly Taylor needed to know exactly what the position was regarding fall off (*Waters v Taylor* (1980) EAT 321/80).

- If you are trying to prove that a dismissal is for union membership or activities, you may want copies of the disciplinary records of other workers, details of management's past relations with and attitude to trade unions, and copies of any blacklists circulated by employers' associations.

  ■ Ms Hyman claimed she was sacked because of her union activities. 'Wrong,' said her employer. 'We sacked you because of continuous absenteeism.' Ms Hyman asked the tribunal to let her have discovery of documents related to the absenteeism of her fellow workers. The chairperson said that she couldn't have them. The onus of proof in a trade union activities case was on the applicant. The EAT overruled this decision. If the documents showed that other workers had been absent more than Ms Hyman it might suggest that she was sacked for some other reason. The documents were therefore relevant and should be produced (*Hyman v Stapeley Home and Hospital* (1981) EAT 288/81).

General Workers Union

31 Westward Road

Brownpool

Dear Sir/Madam,

CASE NUMBER:

We represent our Joan Smith in respect of her claim for unfair dismissal.

Our member is entitled to discovery of the following documents:

1. A copy of her contract of employment.

2. Copies of correspondence, internal memoranda, minutes or other documents relating to her dismissal. The documents should include any documents relating to the disciplinary procedure and/or any investigations into or relating to the circumstances of the dismissal of the acts that led up to it.

3. Copies of the works rules.

4. Documents relating to any pension scheme(s), applicable to our member.

5. Documents relating to the earnings of our member. The said documents should set out the gross and net amounts earned weekly and specify in detail the deductions made.

6. Documents relating to any change in the rate of earnings for our member's former job.

7. Documents relating to any future job prospects.

8. Copies of our member's personnel records.

9. Copies of any training schemes or documents relating to offers of alternative employment.

We need these documents in advance of the hearing in order to prepare a full case. Please confirm that you are prepared to disclose the said documents within 10 days, failing which we shall make an application to the tribunal for an order to compel you to do so.

Yours faithfully

A. O'Fishall

Sample letters: Request for discovery to employer

General Workers Union

31 Westward Road

Brownpool

Secretary to the Industrial Tribunal

Dear Sir/Madam,

RE: JOAN SMITH - CASE NUMBER:

I enclose a copy of a letter I addressed to the respondents herein
with reference to discovery of documents/further particulars.

I have not received the documents/particulars requested and therefore
wish to apply for an order against the respondents.

In the circumstances please accept this letter as an application for
an order that the respondents do within 10 days disclose the requested
documents/provide the requested particulars.

Yours faithfully

A. O'Fishall

cc: Employer

Request for order for discovery of documents

In sex and race discrimination cases generally there *are* more problems of proof and the documentary evidence that you want will be more far reaching so that an employer may contest discovery. The problem then may be legal appeals and delay. The Nasse and Vyas cases took nearly two years on what was a procedural point in preparing the case. However, it is essential to fight here, as it will be almost impossible to prepare an adequate case of discrimination without full disclosure of relevant documentation.

■ Nasse complained to a tribunal of unlawful discrimination against her by the Science Research Council (under the SDA) in not promoting her from clerical to executive officer. Vyas complained of unlawful discrimination (under the Race Relations Act) by British Leyland in not transferring him to another job. In each case another applicant had been appointed. As the cases involved comparison between the individuals and other applicants in terms of qualifications, Nasse asked for discovery of the annual confidential reports of other applicants and the minutes of the local review board which had made recommendations to the central review board which had not promoted her. Vyas asked for disclosure of details of the employment record of other workers interviewed, their personal history forms, personal assessment records, details of commendations together with their application forms for the advertised post. He also asked for disclosure of the completed interview report forms returned by each member of the interview panel in relation to each person interviewed. The tribunal in Nasse's case and, in Vyas's case, the EAT, ordered discovery without the chairperson inspecting the documents. The employers argued that confidence was vital and the disclosure of some of the documents would be a breach of faith and might even lead to industrial trouble. The Court of Appeal and the House of Lords said that the tribunal and the EAT had been wrong to simply allow discovery.

The case should go back to the tribunal for the chair to inspect the relevant documents and decide which, if any, should be disclosed ((1) *Nasse v Science Research Council*; (2) *Vyas v Leyland Cars* (1979) IRLR 465 HL).

The courts in these cases laid down criteria that the tribunals should take into account:

- tribunals must decide whether the confidential documents are **relevant** or **material** to an issue arising in the case. If they are relevant or material, is discovery **necessary** for fairly deciding the case?
- they should decide this by having a chairperson inspect the documents, usually before the hearing to give you time to consider the material. The chair should balance **necessity** against **confidentiality** and consider means by which confidentiality can be preserved, such as covering up, substituting anonymous references, or holding a private hearing.

Every document is relevant 'which it is reasonable to suppose contains information which may, not which must, either directly enable the party either to advance his own case or to damage the case of his adversary (including) a document which may fairly lead him to a train of enquiry which may have either of these two consequences.' (*Compagnie Financiere v Peruvian Guano Co.* (1882) 11 QBD 55 CA.) When they are deciding whether discovery of documents is *necessary* the tribunal will consider whether a refusal of discovery would impede a full and fair hearing by unfairly handicapping one side and ensuring that all the details of the case are not on the table or whether refusal to grant discovery will lead to expensive delays at the hearing if documents have to be asked for and produced at that stage.

Tribunal chairpersons will also take into account what lawyers call *'oppressiveness'*, the time and trouble involved in producing the documents. In one unfair dismissal case the Court of Appeal upheld an EAT decision that a Gas Board should not have to disclose documents alleged to number 60,000, but only a representative sample (*Wilcox v HGS* (1976) ICR 306 CA).

Recent cases have produced mixed approaches.

- Perera claimed he had been rejected for a Civil Service job because of his race and colour. He asked for discovery of documents containing particulars of all the other candidates for this post over a three year period. The employers claimed that this would cover 1,600 candidates with records dispersed over the country and it would be too difficult to collate all this information. The EAT agreed but said that information should be provided insofar as it was still available in respect of the 78 candidates interviewed at the same time as Perera (*Perera v Civil Service Commission* (1980) IRLR 233 EAT).

You can discover documents from the employer by following the procedure outlined above for further particulars. Make sure discovery takes place *before* rather than at the hearing, when you may have to ask for an adjournment. As with further particulars, you write to regional office, and they then place the matter before a regional chairperson. The tribunal will serve the order by sending it to the employer and sending you a copy. **Make sure you fully read and utilise the documents discovered.** The fact, for example, that a time sheet has mistakes and omissions not directly connected with a case may cast doubt on it as evidence.

- As with further particulars, the employer can request an extension of time as long as this is done within the time limit set for discovery.
- The tribunal can issue an order without hearing the employer, but the employer can then apply to set aside or vary the order.
- Unlike further particulars, the tribunal cannot order discovery without a request from one of the parties.
- A person who fails to carry out an order to produce certain documents can be **prosecuted** and **fined** up to £100. The 1980 rules provide a simpler additional sanction. They enable the tribunal to strike out a notice of appearance or dismiss an application where an order for discovery is not complied with. Before they do this, tribunals should allow the party involved to defend themselves by either an oral hearing or written representations.
- We have seen that certain documents prepared for conciliation are 'privileged' and do not need to be disclosed (see page 96). This also applies to letters or documents to trade union officials or legal advisers drawn up in preparation of the case. Communications with other people are 'privileged' if they were intended to obtain information on which legal advice is to be given in connection with a claim. You do *not* need to give the employer documents containing advice or statements of evidence from witnesses.
- Be prepared to pay reasonable copying charges.
- If a relevant document is held by a third party not involved in the case, the tribunal has no power to order discovery. Tribunals encourage both sides to disclose their documentary evidence to each other before the hearing. They send both sides a note (IT4) on these lines. You have little to

lose by co-operating, as your employer will generally possess more documents than you do.

Discovery generally helps the worker more than the employer. **Use it!** Do not rely on the tribunal to discover documents. If you know of their existence it's up to you to ask for them (*Brown v Southall & Knight* (1980) IRLR 130 EAT).

Witness orders

We have looked at the value of witnesses (Chapter 7). According to the tribunal rules, if a witness is unwilling to attend, either side can be granted a witness order or subpoena compelling him or her to come to the hearing, give evidence and bring along any relevant documents. As a general rule, **you should not get a witness order against somebody who is hostile to your case.**

If you call a witness under an order, you will not be entitled to cross-examine him or her. If you force a witness to appear he or she may give evidence which is unhelpful at best or damaging at worst. You will have no opportunity to effectively challenge this evidence. Moreover, a tribunal is unlikely to agree that a witness you have subpoenaed should be treated as a hostile witness. In fact, they will pay great attention to this evidence. If your first thought is to call members of management to embarrass the company, or on the basis that they will cordially tell a story which will damage the employer, **you should think twice**.

However, an order may be useful where somebody is willing to attend but the employer refuses time off, or the worker wishes to seem compelled. A worker may not wish to appear against the employer because of fears of job security or promotion prospects. Action by an employer in these circumstances could lead to legal action – but that might not save the job! Sometimes those fears may not have any basis but they may make a witness hesitate. Shop stewards have been known to ask an employer who is calling them as a witness to get an order, as they do not wish to be seen giving evidence against their members.

A witness may not reply to the request for an undertaking that he will attend. In those circumstances it may be necessary to issue such an order . . . Again he may equivocate or give an answer which at any rate leaves the applicant in reasonable doubt whether the witness will attend in the absence of such an order . . . Finally although not exclusively (because these problems arise in many shapes, forms and sizes) there is the case of the witness who says, 'Certainly I will come and give evidence but it would be very much easier for me to come if I had a witness order requiring me to come'. That situation can arise if an employer is unwilling to release a witness. Again, that would be a reason for granting a witness order (*Dada v Metal Box Co. Ltd* (1974) ICR 559 NIRC).

- **Ask witnesses to attend** as soon as possible after you have sent off the IT1.
- Let them know that **the tribunal can compensate a witness** for travelling expenses, subsistence and loss of wages.
- If you receive no reply and attempts to get in touch fail, it may be wise to **apply for an order**.
- If your **witness fails to turn up**, you have to go ahead in unsatisfactory circumstances, or ask for an adjournment. If you have an order an adjournment will be acceptable. If you haven't it could lead to an award of costs against you.

The procedure for getting a witness order is similar to the procedure for other orders. It may be advisable to send copies of your letters to potential witnesses to the tribunal. If you decide that you need an order apply to the tribunal using the kind of letter on page 145. Explain briefly why you want the witness to attend, the subject matter and relevance of his or her evidence, the fact that she or he is unwilling to attend voluntarily, and, *if relevant*, what documents you would like her or him to produce.

The tribunal can then issue an order.

■ There are only two matters of which tribunals should be satisfied before they issue a witness order. The first is that the witness prima facie can give evidence relevant to the issue in dispute. The second matter of which the tribunal should be satisfied is that it is necessary to issue a witness order (*Dada v Metal Box Ltd* (1974) NIRC).

You do not have to give a full account of what the witness will say. An indication of the subject matter and its relevance is usually enough. But the chairperson may ask for a proof of evidence.

The tribunal can issue an order without any further investigation or hearing. They will draw up a statement of the request and the time and place of attendance. They will also inform the potential witness that failure to turn up can lead to prosecution, with a maximum penalty of £100. This penalty is, of course,

General Workers Union

31 Westward Road

Brownpool

Secretary to the Industrial Tribunal

Dear Sir/Madam,

RE: JOAN SMITH v XYZ LTD - CASE NUMBER:

I represent my above named member.

I wish to apply for a witness order against _____

I enclose copy letters that I have addressed to _____
requesting her/him to attend the hearing.

I understand _____ will not attend before the
Tribunal without a witness order.

I consider that her/his evidence may be necessary to enable me to
conduct my member's case properly in that:

_____ is a witness who is familiar with
the circumstances leading to the dismissal of my member.
She/he can give a detailed account of the two allegedly
'spoiled' jobs which led to the dismissal.

Please order her/him to produce these documents at the hearing. In
the circumstances will you grant the order for a witness summons.

Yours faithfully

A. O'Fishall

cc: Employer

Sample letter: request for witness order

ludicrous but *The Times* (3 June 1977) reported a prosecution against a witness who failed to comply and was fined £10 with £60 costs.

The tribunal will generally send you the witness order, and *you* then send it recorded delivery, or deliver it personally to the witness. You need evidence that you have done so in case the witness doesn't turn up and you want an adjournment. Although tribunal chairpersons often issue orders with no inquiry they can, before they grant you an order, require you to send a notice to the potential witness saying that he or she can object within a time limit laid down by the tribunal. If the person wishes to resist on the grounds, for example, that she or he cannot give relevant evidence, she or he can ask for a preliminary hearing.

- If a witness is victimised because he or she has given evidence against the employer, a case could be taken up in the High Court, which can issue an injunction to prevent interference with the administration of justice (*Attorney General v BBC* (1978) 1WLR 477 HC).
- There is *no* formal procedure through which you can discover which witnesses your opponent will call. You may be able to agree, however, to exchange information on this point.

Another point to remember: if you are dissatisfied with the chairperson's decision on further particulars, discovery or witness orders, you cannot appeal to the EAT. You must ask for a review. The chair's verdict is a *ruling* not a *decision* (*Nikitas v Metropolitan Borough of Solihull* (1981) EAT 639/81).

Questions procedure

As we have seen you may have particular problems if you are taking a sex discrimination or race relations case. A special procedure is laid down to help you decide whether you have a case, and to prepare and present that case. In such cases you need to get hold of Forms SD74 (see page 147) and RR65 from the Job Centre, CRE or EOC. These forms allow you to put a series of formal questions to your employer. These questions and the employer's answers can be produced as evidence in a tribunal hearing. You can use this procedure *before* you complete an IT1.

- If the employer's answers are satisfactory, you may decide that it is not worth taking the case to a tribunal.

THE SEX DISCRIMINATION ACT 1975 SECTION 74 (1)(a)

QUESTIONNAIRE OF PERSON AGGRIEVED (THE COMPLAINANT)

Name of person to be questioned (the respondent)	To	....
Address	of	....
		....
Name of complainant	1.	I ....
Address		of ....
		....

consider that you may have discriminated against me contrary to the Sex Discrimination Act 1975.

Give date, approximate time, place and factual description of the treatment received and of the circumstances leading up to the treatment (see paragraph 9 of the guidance)

2. On

Complete if you wish to give reasons, otherwise delete the word "because" (see paragraphs 10 and 11 of the guidance)

3. I consider that this treatment may have been unlawful because

This is the first of your questions to the respondent. You are advised not to alter it

4. Do you agree that the statement in paragraph 2 is an accurate description of what happened? If not in what respect do you disagree or what is your version of what happened?

This is the second of your questions to the respondent. You are advised not to alter it

5. Do you accept that your treatment of me was unlawful discrimination by you against me?
If not
    a   why not?
    b   for what reason did I receive the treatment accorded to me?
    c   how far did my sex or marital status affect your treatment of me?

Enter here any other questions you wish to ask (see paragraphs 12–14 of the guidance)

6.

Form SD74(a)

Delete as appropriate
If you delete the first alternative, insert the address to which you want the reply to be sent

7. My address for any reply you may wish to give to the questions raised above is *that set out in paragraph 1 above/the following address

See paragraph 15 of the guidance.

Signature of complainant ....

Date ....

NB *By virtue of section 74 of the Act, this questionnaire and any reply are (subject to the provisions of the section) admissible in proceedings under the Act and a court or tribunal may draw any such inference as is just and equitable from a failure without reasonable excuse to reply within a reasonable period, or from an evasive or equivocal reply, including an inference that the person questioned has discriminated unlawfully.*

Form SD74(a) *continued*

THE SEX DISCRIMINATION ACT 1975 SECTION 74 (1)(b)

REPLY BY RESPONDENT

Name of complainant To ....

Address of ....

....

Name of respondent I I ....

Address of ....

....

Complete as appropriate hereby acknowledge receipt of the questionnaire signed by you

and dated .... which was served on me on (date) ....

*Delete as appropriate 2. I *agree/disagree that the statement in paragraph 2 of the questionnaire is an accurate description of what happened.

If you agree that the statement in paragraph 2 of the questionnaire is accurate, delete this sentence. If you disagree complete this sentence (see paragraphs 21 and 22 of the guidance) I disagree with the statement in paragraph 2 of the questionnaire in that

Form SD74(b)

*Delete as appropriate

3. I * accept/dispute that my treatment of you was unlawful discrimination by me against you.

If you accept the complainant's assertion of unlawful discrimination in paragraph 3 of the questionnaire delete the sentences at a, b and c. Unless completed a sentence should be deleted (see paragraphs 23 and 24 of the guidance)

    a My reasons for so disputing are

    b The reason why you received the treatment accorded to you is

    c Your sex or marital status affected my treatment of you to the following extent:—

Replies to questions in paragraph 6 of the questionnaire should be entered here

4.

Delete the whole of this sentence if you have answered all the questions in the questionnaire. If you have not answered all the questions, delete "unable" or "unwilling" as appropriate and give your reasons for not answering.

5. I have deleted (in whole or in part) the paragraph(s) numbered .... above, since I am **unable/unwilling** to reply to the relevant questions of the questionnaire for the following reasons:—

See paragraph 25 of the guidance

Signature of respondent ....

Date ....

SD 74(b)

Form SD74(b) *continued*

● If the employer's answers do not satisfy you, they will help you to decide what is in dispute and what is agreed, as well as giving you basic information to help in preparing the case, and therefore make proceedings simpler and quicker.

If you are sending the questionnaire to your employer before complaining to a tribunal, and you want it to be used later at the hearing, **you must let your employer have the questions within three months** of the incident that you are complaining about.

Even if you feel that you have a definite case, or owing to time limit you have to get the IT1 in quickly, you should send off the questionnaire at the same time as the IT1. If you want the questions and answers to be admissible as evidence in the tribunal, then **you must let your employer have the questionnaire within 21 days** of the tribunal receiving your IT1.

If you are taking a case and this time limit has *expired*, **then you have to obtain written leave** from the tribunal to serve the questionnaire on the employer. You must set out the details of your case and why you want the questions answered. But **you should get your questionnaire off within 21 days**, when there are no whys and wherefores because the tribunal may not grant you an extension of time.

Send the tribunal copies of your questions and the employer's replies, if any, to the tribunal well before the case. If you have them before you send off an IT1, send these as well. The tribunal can draw any inference they wish from the fact that your employer has not replied to your questions or that the replies are inadequate or evasive, including the inference that the employer has committed an unlawful act under the relevant legislation.

■ Virdee, a Sikh, applied for an advertised job as a laboratory technician. At the interview he was asked what nationality the people he had previously worked with were, and if he had any problems supervising white technicians. He did not get the job. He subsequently telephoned one of the managers on the interview panel about another advertised vacancy as a senior technician and was told that he was too well qualified for both jobs and did not have enough experience for the senior position.

He filled in a questionnaire with the help of the CRE listing nine questions on 10 January. The company replied on 18 January, but answered only one of the nine questions. The tribunal accepted evidence from management that they had read and understood the relevant sections of the RRA before replying. They therefore found that the evasion must have been deliberate and that it would be just and equitable to draw the inference that the company had discriminated against Virdee in not selecting him (*Virdee v EEC Quarries Ltd* (1978) IRLR 295).

Many of the same points will apply to the use of questionnaires as will apply to the other methods of getting information from your employer. You should look at the questionnaires and use them in conjunction with the discovery of documents and requests for further particulars. If the questionnaires will give you the information, there may be no necessity for the other mechanisms. **You are not limited to the questions on the form.** For example, para 6 of each form asks you to enter any other questions you want to ask your employer and the *Guidance Notes* say: 'For example, if you think you have been discriminated against by having been refused a job you may want to know what were the qualifications of the person who did get the job and why that person got the job' (*Guidance Notes* para 12).

- John Oxford applied for a clerical job in an office which largely employed women. Of the 17 applicants selected for an interview, 13 were women. Five of the applicants were offered jobs, of whom four were women. Oxford took a case to a tribunal under the Sex Discrimination Act. He sent the employers a questionnaire asking for the names, addresses, sex and age of the successful applicants. He later asked for details of their qualifications. The employers sent him details of sex and ages but not names, addresses or qualifications. He lost his case and appealed on the grounds that he had not been given the relevant information.

  The EAT held that it was ordinarily right to refuse names and addresses. Qualifications were not needed here as all that was required for the job was a minimum qualification of GCE O Levels and all the applicants met this requirement. 'But speaking generally we see no reason why such information as to qualification should not be disclosed and we think that it should be. In applications of this kind it is perfectly simple for the identity of the individual to be concealed under a letter – 'A', 'B', 'C', and for the addresses to be withheld but the other information relevant to the particular case to be disclosed' (*Oxford v DHSS* (1977) ICR 884 EAT).

- **Be as precise as possible** in explaining what happened. You are asking whether or not the employer agrees. It is therefore important to be specific, and tie him or her down. A vague statement will allow the employer to wriggle (para 2).
- If you do not feel able to refer to different statutory kinds of discrimination (para 3) simply **cross out** the 'because'.
- **Read the** *Guidance Notes* carefully before filling them in.
- If you have any problems, **consult the CRE and EOC**, who will have more experience of these questionnaires.

9.

Approaching the hearing

You will usually be given details of the hearing five to seven weeks after your application. This chapter will help with:

- your final preparation;
- postponements and adjournments;
- withdrawal of your case;
- written submissions;
- preparing your documents;
- private hearings;
- defamation and the media;
- arrival at the tribunal; and
- final thoughts before the case commences.

This chapter is mainly aimed at representatives, but also applies if you are bringing your own case.

Where to find the law
Industrial Tribunals Regulations 5, 16, 12(1), 12(2)(b), 12(2)(c), 7(2), 7(1), 17.

Preparation for the hearing

You should finally put your case together and consider its presentation.

Make a detailed note of your facts, arguments and legal points and the order in which you intend to present them. Try to ensure that you know your case in precise detail and have the important times, dates, names and numbers in your head so that you can conduct it without constant reference to notes. Make sure that you have thoroughly read all documents and legal cases.

Have at hand all correspondence relating to the case, any documents to be used as evidence, proofs of evidence, relevant case law and acts, estimates of compensation, details of social security benefits and jobs applied for.

It is sometimes useful to have detailed notes, but break them down to **a brief shorthand outline of the main points** to which you can refer at a glance, being familiar with the subsidiary detail.

Check that your witnesses have copies of their proofs of evidence and any other documents they need, the questions they will be asked and what to expect in cross-examination.

To repeat: It is useful for witnesses who have never attended a hearing to do so before they themselves are personally involved, to get an idea of procedure and atmosphere. This helps to reassure a first-time or nervous witness and can be arranged by a telephone call to the tribunal a week or so in advance. Make clear to all your side that the procedure, with the chairperson taking everything down in longhand, makes the hearing extremely long-winded and creates a very artificial atmosphere for workers to relax in.

Consider the evidence your opponent's witnesses are likely to give and consider *broadly* your own cross-examination (see page 185). *Don't* prepare specific questions for cross-examination. What you ask will depend on what the witness has said in examination. As with preparing the case, put yourself in the employer's position. How would you handle it from the bosses' side? Over-estimate rather than under-estimate the strength of opponents' arguments and the force of their presentation.

If at all possible, **try to have a member attend who will not be directly involved**. As with negotiations, such a member may be able to take a more balanced view of how things are going and will also be able to take full notes.

Stress to your side that you are the orchestra conductor. If they wish to make a point they should neither speak nor wait until the lunch break. They should pass you a note.

Many trade unionists on first appearing before a tribunal worry about their speaking ability. Tribunals want to find out what happened and what the relevant law is. They will not be impressed by the lofty rhetorical style of great advocates attempting to sway juries or of union officials attempting to get their members back to work. Your job is to *persuade* the tribunal. **You are likely to do this by a carefully argued logical approach rather than by harangues or emotional appeals.**

Notice of the hearing

Each regional office of tribunals keeps a detailed record of the way each case progresses from the time it receives the IT1. This provides a detailed record of the preliminaries and what has happened to the case prior to the hearing. The tribunal members will read your application, the employer's reply and any written representations.

After the receipt and exchange of IT1 and IT3 and the use of any preliminary mechanism such as witness orders, discovery of documents or requests for further particulars, the regional office will let both sides know the date of the hearing. **In a normal case the office may:**

(1) Write to the parties five or six weeks in advance of the hearing giving dates, e.g. 8 April 1981 – 14 April 1981. Cases normally take about half a day to hear, and if you think that your case is likely to take longer let them know. As many cases can easily take a day, this point is worth considering.

Similarly, if essential witnesses cannot make any of the dates or if, because of further particulars or discovery, you think the dates are too near, **let the tribunal know**.

(2) You will receive a formal notice of hearing giving you a specific date. **You must be given at least 14 days' notice of when the hearing will take place.**

This notice will point out that you should personally attend, bring relevant documents, and will point out to the employer, in dismissal cases, that he or she may have to give evidence on the availability of jobs in relation to reinstatement or re-engagement.

If you do not propose to attend either personally or through a representative, **you should inform the tribunal in writing**, giving the case number and your reasons. You should also let them know whether you want the case to go on in these circumstances, relying on written representations.

(3) If there are any further changes, the tribunal will again get in touch by letter.

In special circumstances, the tribunal may ask the parties to agree to shorter periods of notice where there are a number of postponements or settlements which leave free periods. If you ask for postponements at this stage there should be no problems but do so quickly and give full reasons, so that it is clear you are not simply using delaying tactics. It may be easier sometimes to get in touch with the other side direct the see which dates are mutually convenient. If you keep on postponing the case there may be problems.

Where the case is heard

A case is heard in England or Wales where the employer 'resides and carries on business', or where 'your cause of action' – the facts which give you the right to take legal action – would have arisen in England and Wales if it had been a County Court action. The case will be heard in Scotland under their rules of procedure if the employer resides or carries on business in Scotland, or the case relates to a contract of employment which was to be performed in Scotland.

- The EAT has said that 'residing in' means having sufficient presence within the area of jurisdiction to be able to receive the originating application (*Odeco UK Inc. v Peacham* (1979) ICR 823 EAT). For companies outside Britain this means registration under the Companies Act 1948 which requires companies with a place of business in Britain to furnish the Registrar of Companies with details. Companies registered in England and Wales or Scotland will be treated as 'resident' there.
- A county court has jurisdiction if the employer resides or carries on business in the court district, or the cause of action arises there. For example, if dismissal takes place in England, then the English tribunals have jurisdiction, even if the company has no registered office there. However, where a dismissal letter was posted in Dublin the tribunal held that a dismissal letter takes effect when posted so that the cause of action arose in the Republic of Ireland, not England (*Tweddell v Irish Shipping Ltd* (1979) COIT 876/76).
- If you work for a subsidiary company which is registered only in Scotland and carries on business only there, the case has to be brought in Scotland, even if the parent company is English (*Kennedy v Christies Scaffolding (Medin) Ltd* (1979) COIT 865/195).
- Cases can be transferred between England and Scotland if the president or regional chairperson has agreed, the case can be more conveniently tried by transfer, and if notice has been sent to all parties allowing them an opportunity to

object. The tribunal to which the case is being transferred must have jurisdiction.

- If you are serving notices and documents on a company which has no registered office in the UK, you can serve the notice abroad with the permission of the regional chairperson.

Interim hearings

The pre-hearing procedure is similar to the normal case except everything is speeded up. The employer is sent a copy of the IT1, the certificate, and the notice of hearing is sent to both you and the employer at this stage. The tribunal does not have the power to postpone unless there are 'special circumstances'. An average hearing will take place two to three weeks after the dismissal. The case will be heard by a chairperson sitting alone, rather than by a full tribunal. For an analysis of procedure see *Forsyth v Frys Metals Ltd* (1977) IRLR 243.

Remember: a tribunal does not have jurisdiction to hear an application for interim relief unless:

- your IT1 is supported by a valid certificate in writing signed by an official authorised by your union for this purpose;
- that certificate states that at the date of your dismissal you were or proposed to become a member of the union and that there were reasonable grounds for supposing that the reason for dismissal related to your union membership or activities.

In *Bradley v Edward Ryde and Son* (1979) ICR 488 EAT, the appeals tribunal stated that in deciding whether a certificate was valid 'too great a concentration on technicality is to be avoided'. What tribunals should look for is a substantial compliance with the requirements of the section. In *Sulemany v Habib Bank Ltd* (1982) EAT 207/82, the EAT endorsed this. In deciding whether there has been substantial compliance tribunals should read the certificate in conjunction with the IT1. It is not essential for a union to authorise expressly an official to act for the purpose of this section. Authority will be presumed in the absence of a challenge from the employer by reason of the official's general functions, but where the official's implied authority *is* challenged, the certificate will be invalid and the tribunal will have no authority to hear your case **unless you can satisfy the tribunal that because**

**of the general job the official does in the union authority should be
implied**.

Postponements

Once a date has been fixed the tribunal may be reluctant to allow
a postponement. This can lead to inconvenient gaps in the tribunals' case schedule and, if the employer is seeking postponement, hardship to the worker who wants a quick result and brass
in pocket. The regulations state that the tribunal can postpone or
adjourn any case, particularly where there is a possibility of a
settlement being reached by conciliation.

A tribunal should allow postponement only where there are
reasonable grounds for exercising their power. Where, for
example, an unfair dismissal case was postponed on the grounds
that it would help the tribunal if a related wrongful dismissal case
being brought in the High Court was heard first, a postponement
was upheld. In the specific circumstances it would make the job
of assessing unfair dismissal compensation much easier if the
tribunal had the judgement of the High Court assessing and
explaining the amount of damages awarded (*Jacobs v Norsalta
Ltd* (1976) 11 ITR 206 EAT). In the majority of cases where the
tribunal case is accompanied by High Court proceedings, the
tribunals have followed this reasoning. However, the decision is
up to the chairperson. The law gives chairpersons

> a complete and wide discretion to postpone or not as they
> think best in the interests of justice . . . it is for the chairman
> in every case to consider the nature and the object of High
> Court or other proceedings for which he is asked to postpone
> the hearing of the application to the tribunal and any abuse of
> postponement proceedings is something which in my judge-
> ment chairmen can be trusted to deal with robustly and clear
> sightedly (Lord Justice Stephenson in *Carter v Credit Change*
> (1979) ICR 913 CA).

■ The employers sacked Carter and sued him in the High Court
for breach of contract. He applied to a tribunal claiming unfair
dismissal. The employers asked for the tribunal hearing to be
adjourned until after the High Court hearing. The tribunal
postponed the case. There would have been an overlap
between the two cases and the facts and issues could be
brought out more rigorously in the stricter High Court pro-

ceedings. This outweighed the problem of delay, particularly as Carter was not asking for his job back. The EAT felt that the issues, fraud and forgery on the one hand, and whether the dismissal was reasonable on the other, were not the same and that speed was the overriding principle, unless there were special reasons. The Court of Appeal restored the tribunal decision; speed was not the overriding principle, it was up to the chairman and he should only be overruled if his decision was an extremely unreasonable one (*Carter v Credit Change*).

The EAT will not interfere with a tribunal's decision to postpone unless it is used in an arbitrary fashion or, 'if a refusal to grant an adjournment involves an injustice to either party' (*Masters of Beckenham Ltd v Green* (1977) ICR 535 EAT). In that case, where an employer's representative failed to turn up because the man handling the case had left the company, the EAT stressed that 'the delay to the employee has to be balanced against the loss to the employer in not being represented'.

Where criminal proceedings arising out of the same situation as the tribunal case are pending, even though the criminal case may take a year to come to trial, you may seek a postponement on the grounds that you could make incriminating or damaging statements in the tribunal proceedings which could be used against you in the later case (see *Wagstaff v The Trade and Industrial Press Ltd* (1968) 3 ITR 1). In Scotland, tribunals always postpone where criminal proceedings are pending.

An overlap situation can also occur where under the RRA or SDA the EOC and CRE are carrying out an investigation into an employer's practices whilst an individual is at the same time bringing a tribunal case alleging discrimination from which she or he has suffered. In *Electrolux Ltd v Goodwin* (1977) EAT 780/77 this happened. The employers asked the tribunal to grant a postponement. The chair refused and they appealed to the EAT which were in favour of granting the postponement. Once the outcome of the EOC investigation was known it might make it easier to settle the tribunal case, but the matter was finally one for the chair.

The tribunals should also deal in a common sense way with postponements. If either side has problems they should not artificially wait for a specific request for postponement or adjournment, but inform the person of their rights.

■ Priddle was claiming a redundancy payment. His union representative who was to take him to the tribunal was taken ill and he could not get there himself. He went to the nearest Labour Exchange and got the clerk there to ring the tribunal. The clerk told the tribunal clerk that Priddle was in his office and explained why he would not be able to turn up. There was no specific request for a postponement and the case went ahead. The High Court decided that it should be re-heard: 'A tribunal is acting wrongly in law if, knowing that an applicant has all along intended to turn up and give evidence . . . and being satisfied, as they must have been, that he was for one reason or another unable to attend they refuse to adjourn merely because he had not asked expressly for an adjournment' (*Priddle v Fisher & Son* (1968) 3 ITR 358 HC).

If there are any other reasons for postponing a case, for example, because you are still pursuing an internal appeal, put in your reasons for postponement quickly. On the other hand if the employer is messing you about, object to postponements which will lead to long delays and inconvenience.

Remember: The tribunals can ask you to pay costs if you seek an adjournment, but if you can argue that it is the other side's behaviour that has led you to do this, costs could be awarded against them (*M (J) v M (K)* (1968) 3 AER 878 HC).

Withdrawal

If for any reason once the procedure has started you wish to withdraw your application, perhaps because new evidence puts a different complexion on your case or because you have reached an agreement with the employer, write to the tribunal explaining the situation. They will then make an order dismissing the case.

By withdrawing the case after setting the legal procedure in motion you are held to have had your bite at the cherry. It would seem on principle that you cannot re-open the dismissed case by re-applying. However, in one case, a tribunal held that a withdrawal did not stop a fresh application within the time limits if there has been no hearing on the merits (*Sidney v Watts Countrymade Foods* (1978) EAT 453/78). Although in another case the EAT held that the second application was 'vexatious', it has also been held that, where a withdrawal has been sent to the tribunal but has not yet been acted on by the tribunal dismissing the case, then it may be re-opened (*Arnak v Bethwin Anodising*

Co. Ltd (1974) COIT 289/57). If you do withdraw the employer can ask for the dismissal order to contain a requirement that you should pay costs and vice versa.

Written submissions

If one side does not turn up at the hearing then their IT1 or IT3 may be treated as written evidence put in on their behalf. In some cases, however, you may wish to consider putting in written statements because you feel a witness cannot or should not attend in person. If you want to produce written statements instead of calling a witness personally, then **you must send them to the tribunal head office not less than seven days before the hearing**. They will then send the documents to the relevant regional office. You *must* be sent copies at the same time as the other side.

■ In one case a witness was called and gave evidence on oath by reading out his proof of evidence. The other side argued that this was a written submission which had not been supplied to them seven days beforehand. It was held that this was not a written submission within the rules. A written submission is sent to the tribunal *in substitution* for evidence on oath. Hence the seven day rule. Here the situation was part of the informality of tribunal procedure and the other side had the possibility of cross examining the witness which they would not have with a written submission (*Hardisty v Lowton Construction Group Ltd* (1973) 8 ITR 603 NIRC).

If these rules are *not* complied with, then it is up to the tribunal whether they allow the written statements as evidence or not. The tribunal must exercise their discretion so that relevant documents are not excluded (*Rosedale Mouldings v Sibley* (1980) IRLR 387 EAT).

■ On the third day of a hearing the employer's counsel put in as evidence two written statements by two witnesses who had failed to attend. The chairperson refused to admit the statements. The right to do so was upheld by the EAT. No notice had been given, there was no opportunity for the other side to bring in written statements countering this evidence, nor to cross examine. It was up to the tribunal, taking all the circumstances into account, to decide (*Lawrence v Newham London Borough Council* (1978) ICR 10 EAT).

The best way to submit a written representation is in the form of an affidavit. An affidavit is a sworn statement signed by an individual who swears to its truth before a solicitor. The idea is that a tribunal gives more weight to a sworn than an unsworn representation. Even if you do this it is *not* as effective as having a witness present whose evidence is likely to be given even greater weight as he or she is subject to cross-examination and questions by the tribunal.

Documents

The regional office attempts to ensure that tribunal members receive copies of all the case documents a week before the hearing, so that they can read them before the hearing and familiarise themselves with the basic details.

- It is useful to **let the tribunal have copies of all the documents that you are going to use** before the hearing to give them a chance to absorb them. If your case is a good one, this can only help, and tribunals have been known to adjourn where many complicated documents are put to them at the last minute. Copies of proofs of evidence, for example, will help the tribunal to follow questioning of witnesses.
- **Make sure that you have thoroughly read and digested all documents** yourself, can quickly recognise them and know how they will be used.
- **Get in touch with the employer.** Agree upon the contents of a bundle of documents so that both sides and the tribunal know exactly which documents are going to be used.
- Agree with the employer **a system of sequence and identification of documents** so that everybody knows when various documents will be used and can easily find them. If each side has its own bundle and system of identification this will lead to delays.
- **Copy documents** for yourself, relevant member witnesses and the employer. Make copies for the three tribunal members.

Note: Tribunals are not bound by the rule that original documents must be produced, but it is always advisable to have these available in case they need to be inspected.

Using your imagination

Think about the kind of documentation that can get your case across to the tribunal and help you to win it. Will a visual diagram of the workplace help? Will photographs make it easier for the tribunal to understand the points you are making? Will it help if you actually bring along as exhibits the implements that were being used or a sample of the materials that were being processed? Tape recordings may be admitted as hearsay evidence subject to the tribunal's discretion (*Jones v Trust House Forte Hotels Ltd* (1977) EAT 58/77). They will, however, take into account the fact that those recorded might not have known they were being taped and might have made statements they would *not* have made with more consideration (*Thompson v Pye Telecommunications Ltd* (1977) COIT 686/88). In many cases today, particularly equal pay or unfair selection for redundancy, an awful lot can turn on the tribunal's understanding of the job done by the applicant and other workers and the set up of the workplace. In one equal pay case the EAT stated that visits to the workplace are useful but that they should come after the basic factual and legal ground has been identified (*Dorothy Perkins Ltd v Dance* (1977) EAT 478/76). Think about this possibility.

Private hearings

Tribunal hearings are normally open to the public, but you or your opponent can **request that the public be excluded** on any of the following grounds:

(1) it is in the interests of national security;
(2) information would be disclosed which would be in breach of an Act of Parliament;
(3) information would be disclosed which has been communicated to one of the parties in confidence;
(4) information would be disclosed which would cause substantial injury to the interests of an undertaking for reasons other than its effect on negotiations between employers and trade unions over collective bargaining matters.

It is unlikely that either side will want a private hearing. If anything, the employer is more likely to wish for confidentiality than you are. **From your point of view, publicity may be an advantage.** In the unlikely event of *wanting* a private session, you should apply to the tribunal giving a *full* statement of reasons.

A preliminary hearing may be necessary if the other side challenges the necessity for such a step. Evidence at the preliminary hearing may disclose the points the party wants to keep confidential so that a chairperson can decide that the tribunal should sit in private *at this stage*. The public would be admitted to hear the decision as to privacy and then excluded for the full hearing. As decisions are open to the public, the reasons for the decision may be omitted from entry on the Register if the tribunal thinks that this might cause problems.

■ Maurice Cahm was sacked by his employers for photocopying and distributing copies of documents which allegedly showed how the company got around the exchange control laws of other countries when foreign purchasers paid them for their products. The tribunal agreed to the employer's request that the hearing should be in private as the documents were confidential and their disclosure might cause problems to the company (*Cahm v Ward and Goldstone Ltd* (1979) ICR 574 EAT).

A decision on whether or not there should be a private hearing is for a full tribunal *not* the chairperson. **There have been private hearings:**

- where details were to be disclosed about a burglar alarm installation (*Neal v Christie Intruder Alarms Ltd* (1976) COIT 549/115);
- where evidence was to be given about matters contained in police reports (*Wilson v Crown Office* (1976) COIT F61/4).

The media

If you wish to use the tribunal as a platform to draw attention to the behaviour of a particular employer you have to be careful. No matter how many safeguards you take you may get no more truthful an account printed than you get of strikes or union meetings. If you *do* feel that press or local radio coverage would be useful then you may be able to have an advance press release issued as well as coverage of the hearing and interviews afterwards. You should look at Denis MacShane's book, *Using the Media* (Pluto Press). Brief your side as to who, if anybody, will deal with the press and on what lines.

Defamation

Can you be sued for libel or slander because of verbal or written statements you make during a tribunal case? You will be *absolutely* protected against legal action in relation to any testimony you give at a tribunal hearing and you will be protected against action in relation to written statements or statement to conciliation officers or advisers, *unless* it can be shown that you deliberately made the statements knowing that they were false with the intention of injuring, say, your former employer.

Adjournments

We have looked at the rules applying to adjournment, i.e. breaks once the case has started, under postponements. If you run into practical problems during the hearing, consider asking for an adjournment. For example, you may realise that you need a particular document or that you want to call a witness on a particular important point. If the tribunal feels that there is no reason why you could not have dealt with this point prior to the hearing they can refuse an adjournment or grant it, but you will have to pay costs (see page 207). If you can justify an adjournment they may grant it. The practical problem is that if there is an adjournment of this kind it may be difficult to find another convenient day for the case and this would lead to delays and hardship for the other side.

■ In one case there was still a lot of ground to cover after hearings had taken up three days in June and July. It was adjourned on the request of the employers' counsel to an agreed date in September. The barrister then found that he had an important prior engagement on that date and the employers requested a further adjournment until October. The tribunal refused this on the ground that the initial request had come from the employers and there was no date in October on which all three tribunal members could sit.

On appeal it was said that in deciding on an adjournment a tribunal should consider the interests of both parties and the possibility of an injustice to one. Here, they felt that the employers would suffer an injustice if they had to change barristers in mid-stream. The evidence here was technical and lengthy so the adjournment should be granted. On the other hand the worker was being kept dangling on a string and might suffer financial problems. Tribunals should consider adjournments with costs in these types of cases.

You can always raise the question with the tribunal. **It is better to have an adjournment rather than lose the case.** Always consider the balance of convenience to your side if your opponents request an adjournment. Tribunals are very accommodating about short adjournments *within* a hearing to briefly consider a point.

You may also meet problems with a long case.

■ A hearing took place on four separate days over a period of three and a half months, despite repeated requests by the worker's side for hearings on *consecutive days*. They argued that evidence given on earlier days was becoming confused or forgotten and that the split and protracted procedure militated against a fair and just hearing. The High Court said that: 'As many steps as possible ought to be taken so that consecutive hearings may be obtained . . . The real answer is that it cannot be helped particularly in the case of tribunals such as this which include part-time members' (*Barnes v BPC (Business Forms) Ltd* (1975) 10 ITR 110 HC).

At the tribunal

Arrive early so that you can handle any preliminaries or last minute problems. You should also have impressed on the rest of your side the importance of punctuality. Let the tribunal staff know that you have arrived. Normally, they will approach you and note your arrival on a standard sheet. From this you will be able to see if your opponents and any witnesses have arrived.

Identify the employer's representative, if you did not know previously. If it is a lawyer rather than a member of management, this may give you some idea about their attitude and the likely approach in conducting the case. If you are still thinking in terms of a settlement you may wish to discuss this. Make a written note so that you will know how to refer to the adviser during the hearing.

Look at the employer's witnesses. If you are not already aware of these details, it may give you some indications as to how your opponent's case will be argued. If a potentially important witness is not present, this might mean that the employer is on the defensive and is prepared to concede your version of events, or is going to take a different tack in argument and presentation.

See that your own witnesses have arrived. Your side will be conducted into a waiting room (separate from your opponent's) and your job will be to reassure them, try to relax them and clear up any last minute points.

Check the timing of the case. You may have been asked to come at 10.00 a.m., but find two cases down for hearing before yours by the same tribunal. These may only be short technical hearings so don't get too flustered. If there are delays, use the time by going over the case with your witnesses.

Contact the clerk to the tribunal. The clerk will normally introduce her or himself. He or she is not legally qualified but is rather like a court usher. The job is to see that tribunal members are supplied with all documents, exhibits, cases and so on, to call witnesses, administer the oath, provide claim forms, explain any problems to the parties and generally make matters run smoothly. If you have any questions or problems, let him or her know. An experienced clerk will often have a detailed knowledge of what goes on in tribunals.

Give the clerk the address of the Department of Health and Social Security or Department of Employment office from which you received payment of benefit. This is to enable the DHSS or DoE to recoup any unemployment or supplementary benefit paid to you between dismissal and the hearing from the compensation awarded to you if you win (see page 219).

Check the listing sheet. You will generally find a typed sheet pinned up on a notice board listing the cases to be heard that day and the names of the tribunal members. No details of their background are given, however. The clerk may be prepared to give you information or at least identify the union representative, but is under no obligation to do so. If you feel that any member has connections with the case which might prejudice the hearing, let the clerk know. If there is no tribunal member free to exchange places with the challenged member, the case can be postponed or, if both sides agree, a tribunal may sit with only one lay member. If you have a marginal case where the member has a slight connection, you have to weigh up the advantages and disadvantages of a postponement.

Inform the clerk, if you have not done so previously, of any cases you will be citing so that the clerk can provide copies for the tribunal and the other side. Ask to see the list of authorities the other side are citing. If you do not already know them ask for copies.

If witnesses have not turned up – use the public telephone you will find in the building. Let the clerk know. If the witness is important, explain why you may have to ask for an adjournment.

Explain to your witnesses the basic procedure, if you have not done so before. In England and Wales they will be able to sit through the full hearing unless either side asks for them to be excluded. In Scotland the practice, normal in other courts, is for witnesses to be excluded until the time comes for them to give evidence Ensure they all have pens and paper.

Check that you have all the basic documentation, copies of Acts of Parliament, codes and cases; insert markers at the appropriate pages.

The period before the case starts should be one of checking on last minute details and doing things you should have done earlier.

- A tribunal will normally sit from 10.00 a.m. to 4.00 p.m., with an hour's adjournment for lunch. 'No Smoking' is the rule during the hearing.
- Witnesses go into a witness box and take the oath or affirm.
- It is simplest to address the tribunal members by their ordinary names, although the proper way of addressing the chairperson is 'sir' or 'madam'. 'Chairperson' would not be out of place. Make a written note of the names at the start.
- A record of the hearing is not taken down in shorthand. The only official record is provided by the chairperson's notes, which are then used as the basis for the decision. It is vital to have your own record of what occurred, particularly for a review or an appeal. Make sure that somebody on your side takes full notes.

Some general guide lines

Initial nervousness is natural and provides the nervous energy for a concentrated effort. **Find the right vocal pitch and volume for the room, and try to vary your language and tone to avoid monotony. Speak clearly and distinctly.** This is where you will find the benefit of patient preparation. The tribunal will be concentrating on the facts and any legal points, not on your speaking ability or command of English. Careful explanation and precise details are the hallmark of good tribunal presentation. Somebody once pointed out 'the successful lawyer is not often a first-class speaker'.

Talk slowly and distinctly. You should be familiar with all aspects of the case. The tribunal will not be. Take time to explain each matter in detail to people who may have no first-hand experience of particular work situations or trade union practices. **Pause occasionally to let points sink in.** Remember that even experienced listeners can only take in so much detail or argument at one time and that this will be the first time that the tribunal will have heard much of what may be complex and confusing evidence.

As with negotiation, however, you must **be a good listener**, otherwise you will miss key points. There is a certain technique to presenting a case *and* listening carefully. You must not be concentrating so much on what you are going to ask the witness that you miss what she or he is actually saying. Neither can you allow your preparation of what you thought might happen or wanted to happen obscure what is actually happening.

That is why **you should not prepare too rigorously in terms of tactics**. You should try to broadly anticipate the kind of evidence your opponent's witnesses will give and the kind of questions you will want to ask in cross-examination. But if you write down beforehand the precise questions you are going to ask with supplementary questions if the answer is A, and different supplementaries if the answer is B, you will find it extremely difficult to adapt flexibly when the evidence turns out to be different to your forecast.

Arguing before a tribunal is different from many kinds of negotiation. You will not be able to break in, take five minutes off or bang the table. The cut and thrust, forthright language and informality of many negotiating situations is missing. It is much more difficult to 'make contact' with the tribunal than with a manager sitting across the table. The emotional distance is greater. Most importantly the magic ingredient, bargaining power, is missing.

You have to **try to adapt to this situation** if you are to persuade the tribunal and win your case. You will *not* be able to show your feelings or use tactical impatience, annoyance, disgust or disbelief in the way you can whilst negotiating. Nor should you be too scathing as to your opponent's case.

Remember at all times that whether you like it or not you have to **convince these three people that you are right according to certain legal rules**. Knowing that you are right in terms of trade union principles is not enough. You have to be calm, and mould and use your emotional involvement, remembering that winning – not self-justification – is the name of the game. Project a profile throughout of weighed and balanced views. Concede that your opponent has a point if not a case. Accept that alternative views are sincerely held though, you will argue, wrong. Concessions and hesitations lend an aura of truth and balance to your case.

Try to show confidence in your case. Let the tribunal see that you believe in it. The worried, unsure representative will not get across to the tribunal that the case is a good one. If you are clear, assured and methodical the tribunal will be convinced by what you are saying. Once more, careful preparation gives you confidence.

Try to put your case across in a lively and interesting way, but do so by argument relevant to the law. Do not use general arguments on injustice and exploitation – you have no audience – or give your personal opinions on the matters at issue. Nobody is interested.

Humour is useful – if it comes off. If it doesn't you fall flat on your face. Remember your sense of humour may be very different from that of the tribunal members.

Never lose your temper or show that you are taken aback, as this can lead to loss of control of your case. Never confuse lung power with arguing power.

Stick to the main road of your case. Do not wander off down interesting bye ways dealing with subsidiary points which can simply be a waste of time.

Always **adopt a courteous and patient manner**. The style of 'I would submit' or 'I would suggest' is more tailored to the art of gentle persuasion required in tribunal hearings than categorical definite assertions or demands. Whilst in negotiations a frontal assault can pay dividends, here a style of subtle seduction is more likely to be fruitful.

Don't talk too much. Know when to rest your point, argument and whole case. You want the tribunal to see the wood for the trees. Be brief, straightforward and to the point.

10.

The tribunal hearing

This chapter is written for representatives, workers representing themselves, and those helping with a tribunal case. The chapter:

- gives a blow-by-blow account of how an average tribunal case develops;
- gives you advice and examples as to how you can maximise your performance at each stage;
- shows you how to deal with difficult problems; and
- helps you to place yourself in a winning position.

If you are representing yourself, you should get more help from the tribunal than if you are a representative. They will give some help to a non-legal representative but expect you to know the basic rules of procedure.

Where to find the law
Industrial Tribunals Regulations 7, 8, 12.

Procedure at the hearing

In an average case the proceedings will go like this:

(1) The employer makes an **opening statement**.
(2) The employer calls his or her first witness. Each witness takes the oath or affirms. The employer asks the witness questions. This is called the **examination** or **examination in chief**.
(3) You or your representative then **cross-examines**, i.e. gets the opportunity to ask relevant questions about what the witness has said.
(4) The tribunal members, if they feel it necessary, ask the witness questions about the evidence he or she has just given.
(5) If the employer feels that it is necessary, he or she can come back and **re-examine** the witness. If, for example,

basic matters have become confused or new points have arisen from the cross-examination.

(6) You or your representative makes an **opening statement**.

(7) You call your first witness and the **above procedure** is followed.

(8) You make your **final statement** to the tribunal, summarising your case.

(9) The employer makes a **final statement**. ..

(10) There may be some **discussion** as to remedies. This is often discussed after the decision.

(11) The tribunal **adjourns** to discuss the decision.

(12) The tribunal returns and announces its **decision**.

Then there may be discussion of remedies, though the tribunal can leave the parties themselves to negotiate the details of compensation, having laid down broad guidelines. Sometimes if the employer wants time to consider an order of reinstatement or re-engagement, the hearing may be adjourned (see page 200). However, never plan too rigidly for a fixed order and be prepared to be flexible.

Who goes first?

The normal rule in unfair dismissal cases is that the employer goes first (*Gill v Harold Andrews Sheepbridge Ltd* (1974) IRLR 109 NIRC). This is still true under the Employment Act 1980 as the employer still has to prove that there was a statutory reason for dismissal even though the burden is no longer on the employer to prove that the dismissal was reasonable.

- If there is a dispute as to *whether* a dismissal has taken place (constructive dismissal cases) the worker's side goes first. *You* have to prove that a dismissal took place. If the employer is arguing that the contract is 'frustrated', as in some sickness cases, she or he goes first (*Marshall v Harland & Wolff Ltd* (1972) IRLR 90 NIRC).

- Where you admit the reason for dismissal (e.g. redundancy) but dispute the reasonableness, the employer would still normally go first as he or she has knowledge of why the worker was dismissed in a particular way.

- In redundancy payment cases you have to prove dismissal. If you do, the dismissal is presumed to be by reason of redundancy and the employer goes first.

- With the anti-discrimination statutes, you go first.
- With employment protection rights, you go first.
- If the complaint is out of time, you have to prove that there is a good excuse, so you go first.
- If you have less than 52 weeks' service (104 weeks in small firms) and are claiming dismissal on trade union grounds, you go first.
- With jurisdictional questions, e.g. whether you have sufficient continuous employment to qualify, or whether you normally work in the UK, you go first.

The tribunals, however, have a degree of flexibility in the way they handle this matter.

■ Rump claimed unfair dismissal by Hawker Siddeley. The company claimed he resigned. The tribunal found that there had been a dismissal and that it was unfair. One of the questions on appeal was whether the chairman was wrong to ask the employers' representatives to open the case, given that the dismissal was contested. The EAT said: 'it was the reverse of what normally takes place in the circumstances where there is in issue the question of dismissal. However, we remind ourselves that by para 11 of the Rules of Procedure "subject to the provisions of these rules a tribunal may regulate its own procedure" we would not wish it to be thought that anything we say would lead to any departure from the normal procedure. But in this case where there appeared before the tribunal the parties in person, we cannot see that there is any irregularity in asking the employers' representative to put the Tribunal in the picture by going though all the facts so far as they were aware of them' (*Hawker Siddeley Power Engineering v Rump* (1979) IRLR 425 EAT).

If this reversal is to the *detriment* of either side, the position may be different.

■ In another case a worker was made to go first, even though the employer had admitted dismissal. Both employer and worker agreed that this should not have happened as it put the burden of proof on the worker. The EAT agreed that the cases should be reheard by a different tribunal (*Hobbs v GKS Nuts and Bolts* (1979) EAT 133/79).

Opening the case

Until now the tribunal regulations have specifically given each side the *right* to make an opening statement. Arguing that there is a need to make tribunal procedure more informal, the government, in the 1980 tribunal regulations, have abolished this right. Whether or not you can make a tribunal statement is now at the discretion of the tribunal.

Most tribunals will normally allow each side to make a short opening statement. **If you follow the advice below you are unlikely to be stopped.**

The tribunal members will usually sit at a table on a slightly raised dais. You will sit at one side of a table in the main body of the room with the employer's people at the other side. There will be several rows of chairs at the back for members of the public. Sometimes these will not be occupied but you may have a full audience if there are, for example, members of a trade union or management course observing the hearing.

Remember: At the start of the hearing:

- make sure that you have all your documents set out on the table in order of use and in such a way that you can easily refer to them;
- introduce yourself, your member and any witnesses to the tribunal at the start;
- if there are any preliminary matters, time limits, qualifications, etc. which have not been previously dealt with, these should be raised right at the start.

An opening statement is useful because it gives you the chance to:

- break the ice and get your personality across;
- familiarise the tribunal with the basic issues, your basic line of argument, and the structure of your case;
- get across to your witnesses the structure their evidence will hopefully fall into;
- knock your opponent back a little, if you are forceful and confident.

Your opening statement should be short and clear. It should be an outline giving the skeleton of your case. Leave the flesh until later. Do *not* give the detailed arguments you may use later. Do *not* give the detailed evidence your witnesses will give later.

In most tribunal cases you can be very brief. For example:

This is a case where I shall try to persuade the tribunal that an unfair dismissal occurred. Mr O'Neil worked for his employers for five years. As far as the union is concerned, at the time of the incident leading up to the dismissal, he had a clean record. Mr O'Neil was dismissed for refusing to obey an order to leave a shop stewards' meeting and return to work.

I shall call evidence to show that it was customary for Mr O'Neil to have time off to attend these meetings, and that on this particular occasion he had followed the jointly agreed procedure to secure time off.

We shall try to show that in the circumstances it was unreasonable for the employers to retract their permission to attend the meeting in which Mr O'Neil was in fact playing an important part, and unreasonable of them to push their order to the point of dismissal. In fact, there appears to be some doubt as to the reason why Mr O'Neil was recalled, and Mr O'Neil's refusal to return to work was, I shall show, understandable in the circumstances. Even if you accept that an act of misconduct *did* take place, I will try to convince you that dismissal was in all the circumstances too severe a penalty and that the employers' behaviour was unreasonable.

You are outlining the contours of your case, not giving chapter and verse at this stage. If you want to go further, in the context of the above statement, you can refer specifically to the witnesses you will call to demonstrate your assertions and the documents you will introduce as evidence.

- An alternative approach is to briefly state the facts, then comment upon them, segregating facts from comments, whereas in the example given above they are interwoven. To illustrate:

It was the practice for management to allow Mr O'Neil to attend shop stewards' meetings of the kind we will describe. He followed the correct procedure for time off to attend such a meeting. Management attempted to rescind that permission in the middle of the meeting. Mr O'Neil refused to return to work and was dismissed. These are the bones of this case. We shall seek to argue . . .

- Another explanation of your case is the more open – 'These are the issues' approach:

The essence of the problem is this: Has the employer at the last minute the right to abruptly recall a worker who is in the middle of exercising a right to time off? Has the employer the right to sack in these circumstances without even explaining to the worker that he or she will dismissed unless the order is obeyed?

Whichever approach you take, only sketch the bones. If you start giving a blow-by-blow account of the facts at this stage, the tribunal will become impatient and eventually stop you. You will not be off to a very good start. Similarly, do not start bringing in legal cases or referring to the Code of Practice at this stage – leave that to your summing up.

Experienced advocates argue that it is useful at the start to briefly mention any weaknesses in your case and mention that you think they are not in fact crucial weaknesses. This deprives the employer of surprise and impact which might help him if he introduces the point later on.

For example:

The employers will no doubt argue that but for a technicality, Mr O'Neil would have received a written warning for his absence in January. We shall seek to convince the tribunal that it should deal in hard facts not 'ifs' and 'might have beens'. No such warning *was* received.

Or:

I accept that it is arguable that in the best of all possible worlds he should have returned to work there and then, and taken the matter up through the grievance procedure, and that the other union representatives should have advised this. We shall call witnesses who will describe the confused position and show that in the circumstances Mr O'Neil's reaction was quite understandable.

Apart from pulling the rug from under your opponents, this approach shows that you have thought over the case and are taking a balanced view. If you have only told half of the story – the half helpful to you – rest assured that when the other side brings up the other points, they will come across with more force and freshness.

In your opening statement you should start correcting the speed at which you talk. **Follow the chairperson's pen to get the**

pace right as she or he will be taking long-hand notes.

Once more: **do not ramble.**

Examination

There is no set order in which witnesses have to be called: you may do it chronologically; you may call witnesses who can describe background facts first then the applicant; or you may call the applicant first to give the core testimony, and then call other witnesses to document and develop certain points. You have to calculate **which order is going to make the most powerful impression on the tribunal**. A chronological order is often best.

■ In one case the solicitor for the worker's side was instructed by the chairperson against his opposition to call certain witnesses out of order on the grounds that if they were not heard at a particular time their absence from work (they were on a witness order) would cause inconvenience to their employer. On appeal Phillips J. said: 'representatives are entitled to conduct the proceedings as they see fit within the rules and, in particular, to call witnesses in the order they wish . . . It was an unwise decision for the chairman to have made and should not be repeated' (*Barnes v BPC* (1975) 10 ITR 110 HC).

However, the 1980 regulations give the tribunal greater power, so that in appropriate cases they might direct the order of witnesses and this case might not be followed.

The witness makes much more impact if encouraged to tell the story in his or her own words in answer to your questions and if the examination appears to be a natural spontaneous dialogue between you and your witness. The main bones of your case should come from your examination of the witnesses. You should be clearly aware what facts you want your witnesses to testify to, exactly what points you want them to make.

Know your case so well that you do not have to keep sorting through papers to know the next question that you should be asking. We have said that witnesses may be allowed to read from notes but not usually. The other side can object that they do not have as much time to absorb information and think on their feet compared to the question and answer format. The tribunal too likes to see what she or he really remembers and her or his reactions.

- When you have called a witness, get him or her to **tell the story in the order things happened**. If, for example, she or he witnessed a fight between the applicant and a foreman you might want to draw out:
  (1) who the witness is and what is his or her job, and relationship to both sides;
  (2) how the witness came to be on the scene;
  (3) exactly what she or he saw before the fight started;
  (4) exactly what he or she could recall of the fight itself;
  (5) what she or he saw and heard afterwards;
  (6) what she or he knew of the background and temperament of the two combatants and the relationship between them.

- **Do not** simply say to the witness: 'Tell us about the fight in your own words'. Some witnesses *will* be able to give an orderly relevant detailed account. *Most will not.* They will ramble, miss points, or run out of steam. You know what the relevant points you want are. **Direct the witness to the point by questions** then leave him or her to describe the situation in his or her own way.

When the witness has made the point, or is avoiding it, or is rambling, or has not grasped the question, you need to **control the situation so that you will get a precise orderly account.** Pull the wandering witness back to relevancy, slow down one who is talking too fast, encourage one who is nervous or hesitant. If you let the witness rattle on after a satisfactory answer, the tribunal may intervene.

- **Take your time.** Your watchword in all questioning should be 'easy and slow'. **Pause to let answers sink in.**
- Point out that the witness should **direct answers to the tribunal**, not to you.
- You should have planned your examination questions in detail in advance. Keep them short, simple and in logical sequence. **Do not leap from one disconnected point to another,** you will simply confuse the tribunal.

Bad:

Representative: Did Smith and Jones get on well together? How long had they worked together? Had there ever been any trouble between them before? Was Jones annoyed by the fact that Smith had just become branch secretary when he supported Brown?

Better:

Representative: How long had Smith and Jones worked together?
Witness: Approximately five years.
Representative: Had there been any previous problems between them?
Witness: Yes, particularly over the recent election for branch secretary.
Representative: Could you tell us briefly what these problems were?

Questions should be brief and asked one at a time with each question either clarifying information given in the answer or developing and building on it.

Keep your language straightforward.

Bad:

Representative: Further to that lamentable and distressing occurrence and having weighed the alternative variants, what course of action did you feel it incumbent on your good self to undertake?

Better:

Representative: What did you do next?

- Your witness will, initially at least, be nervous. **Be sympathetic and patient. Do not assume that your witness will dovetail with you in a well-synchronised double-act.** Witnesses often forget details that you have thoroughly discussed before the hearing once they are in the box. Pick up any omissions. If the manager said to the steward: 'I'm sorry Jill, we are not starting him. Black workers in that section would cause all sorts of problems', and the witness simply says, 'At the end of the discussion he said I'm not starting him', ask 'What reason did he give?' or 'Can you remember *exactly* what he said?' rather than the leading 'Didn't he also say, 'Black workers . . .'
- **Do not repeat everything your witness says.** This can annoy and irritate the tribunal. On the other hand, if the witness

gives a rather long-winded or messy account, you might isolate the important core by repetition. Similarly, if the piece of evidence is crucial, give the witness a chance to emphasise or amplify the point her or himself: 'Are you quite sure that it happened just like that . . .'

You are doing well . . . when the story emerges in a complete and logical way in the witnesses' own words with minimum guidance from the representative. This is alive and convincing.

Don't forget: You may have touched on weak points in your opening statement. Bring these points out frankly in examination of witnesses. If you leave these aspects to be brought out by the other side in cross-examination, they are likely to leave an impression more damaging to your case.

Representative: What was Mr Campbell's reaction to Ms Harford's order?
Witness: He appeared surprised and annoyed.
Representative: What did he reply to Ms Harford?
Witness: Something like: 'Why don't you do it your fucking self.'
Representative: Was that kind of language common in the shop?
Witness: Yes, people often swore in the presence of the supervisor without the matter being taken too seriously.

Here you are **minimising and trying to play down** something the other side may use. Similarly, if you think that your opponents may try to discredit your witnesses take the bull by the horns:

Representative: Sorry to have to ask you this Ms Jones, but have you ever been sacked by the company?
Witness: Yes.
Representative: Some time ago?
Witness: About seven years ago. After representations by the union the company accepted that the penalty was too harsh, so I received a final written warning which it was agreed was the relevant punishment.
Representative: Since then . . . ?
Witness: I've had a clear record.

By bringing this point out but by dealing with it sympathetically and suggesting the price has been paid, you take the sting out of the employer's attempt to use this in cross-examination, putting the best face on the facts yourself.

Leading questions

Sometimes representatives make a statement then simply ask their own witness to confirm 'yes' or 'no', or frame the question in such a way that the witness will understand the answer that he or she is expected to give. This is known as 'leading the witness'. The rule in the ordinary courts is that, except upon facts which are not disputed between the two sides, the representative must not ask leading questions. Industrial tribunals are not bound by these strict rules of evidence but it is best not to ask leading questions. They will reduce the impact and credibility of the witness's evidence. They make clear that you are putting answers in the witness's mouth and stop him or her coming across fully. Most importantly, 'ifs', 'buts', and contradictions may come out under cross-examination. If there is a conflict of evidence, who are the tribunal going to believe: the witness who naturally and vividly describes a situation in answer to questions or the witness who has his or her evidence read out by the representative and comes across as a spoonfed stooge?

Limit the leading questions to:

(1) introductory matter – name, address, job, union, position;
(2) matters which are not disputed;
(3) trying to get a specific denial of a particular allegation;
(4) helping a nervous or inarticulate witness start off.

Bad:

Leading question: When Applegarth came up, Robinson put Hyde's clock card back in the rack and said, 'What are you looking at you nosey bugger?'?
Still leading: Did Robinson put Hyde's clock card back and swear at Applegarth when he approached?

Better:

The best way to avoid leading questions is to ask a series of short, simple questions:

Representative: What was Robinson doing?
Witness: As I looked up he was standing with a clock card in his hand.

Representative: Was anybody else present?
Witness: Applegarth came walking into the room.
Representative: What did Robinson do?
Witness: He turned around and replaced the clock card in the rack.

Bad:

Representative: I'm going to ask you now about the fight on 13 January. Would it be true to say that on that day Thomas was doing a rush job that the foreman wanted by lunchtime and that when Harvey came up to his machine and asked him if he could spare half an hour to discuss the stewards' meeting he said, 'Bugger off I'm busy'?
Witness: Yes.
Representative: Is it correct that Harvey then said, 'When are you going to start behaving like a shop steward? You are nothing but a gaffer's man', and that Thomas replied, 'I'll give you two seconds to push off' – at which point Harvey punched Thomas who fell backwards against the machine?
Witness: Yes, that's exactly right.

Better:

Representative: I'm going to ask you now about the fight on 13 January. Was there anything unusual about Thomas's schedule that morning?
Witness: Yes, the foreman had asked him to have a rush job completed by lunch time. I know that because he asked me first but agreed that I was too busy.
Representative: When did you first see Harvey that morning?
Witness: I walked back from the canteen at the teabreak with him. He stopped at Thomas's machine to discuss the stewards' meeting we had been talking about over tea.
Representative: What did you do?
Witness: I stopped at the machine myself as I was interested.
Representative: What happened then?
Witness: Thomas appeared unfriendly.
Representative: What did he say?
Witness: Something like, 'You can bugger off I'm busy'.

Introducing documents

You will want to bring in documentary evidence during your examination of witnesses. In asking your question, refer the witness to the relevant page in the bundle, a copy of which the witness should have (see pages 82 and 162).

If no bundle has been prepared, give the witness, the other side and the tribunal members copies and, depending on what it is, you, the chairperson, or the witness may read it. You can then ask for comments or explanations. The document will become part of the evidence and be marked for reference by the chairperson.

Hearsay and direct evidence

An ordinary court accepts as evidence what a witness says that she or he saw or heard him or herself. They will *not* accept what another person told the witness that she or he heard or saw. This second-hand evidence is called hearsay evidence. The difference between hearsay and direct evidence is shown below.

Direct evidence

Representative: Where were you at the time?
Witness: Sitting in the convenor's office writing up the minutes.
Representative: Did you overhear the conversation?
Witness: I was interested so I stopped and listened.
Representative: What did Smith say?
Witness: 'Ms Jones has just told me that I'm dismissed.'

Hearsay evidence

Representative: Had relationships between X and Y been good?
Witness: No. About a year ago they had a stand up row in the canteen.
Representative: Were you there?
Witness: No, but Joe Public told me about it.

Hearsay evidence *can* be admitted by an industrial tribunal. If you want it to be excluded then you must object. Tribunals often allow such evidence, as they want to gain a complete picture of the situation and it just may illustrate an important point.

■ Mr and Mrs Matthews were sacked from their jobs as manager and senior receptionist at the Gateshead Squash Club for allegedly serving drinks after hours. The tribunal decided that the dismissals were unfair. The employers did not have reasonable grounds for suspecting that the offences were committed. They refused to hear evidence from a replacement manager as to complaints made to him about the way the club was being run, on the grounds that it was hearsay. The EAT said that they should have listened to the evidence. A tribunal should have before it evidence which was before the employer when he took the dismissal decision and a substantial part of *that* information *was* the complaints made to the replacement:

The fact that customers who made the complaints could more easily have been produced at the hearing was it seems to us a matter of weight; a matter also to be considered in the context of whether the employers had acted reasonably in following up mere reports and not going to the complainants themselves. It seems to us clear that a tribunal is not bound by the strict rules of evidence but should exercise its good sense in weighing the matters which come before it (*Coral Squash Clubs Ltd v Matthews and Matthews* (1979) IRLR 390 EAT).

So the attitude of tribunals to hearsay evidence should be 'Let us hear what is said and let us see whether or not it is the sort of evidence which may be germane and relevant and may make a difference to the findings of facts' (*Rowland v O'Connor Thompson & Co Ltd* (1978) EAT 221/78).

You must point out to the tribunal that what they are hearing is *hearsay* and should not be treated as *the real thing*. Where there is a dispute, first-hand evidence will obviously *always* override hearsay evidence.

The industrial relations manager, Smith, says that she dismissed Jackson because the superintendent told her that Jackson was drunk and swore at him. If Johnston, who was present, states that Jackson was not drunk and did not swear at the superintendent, then only Johnston, Jackson and the superintendent can testify to the truth of what *did* happen. The manager's evidence is *second-hand* (hearsay). You should cross-examine on what attempts were made to see whether the story was true and, when summing up, point out that, *had it* been investigated, the manager could have reached different conclusions because of Johnston's evidence, of which she was ignorant. Such an objection on these facts would fail because Smith is testifying to her *beliefs*, which is relevant to the *reason* for dismissal.

- **If you are faced with hearsay evidence**, ask why the person who was directly involved has not been called as a witness.
- **If you yourself are introducing hearsay**, then explain to the tribunal *why* you are doing so and why the person directly involved cannot appear.

■ Etherington was sacked and told that his job was to be filled by a younger man. He was not replaced. He applied for a redundancy payment and was opposed, not by the employer, but by the Department of Employment. The tribunal accepted hearsay evidence (obtained from a director who did not appear) that the intention was to replace him. The High Court accepted that the burden of proof on the employer of showing that there was no redundancy situation had not been discharged. The tribunal was wrong to find that he was not redundant on the basis of this evidence (*Etherington v Henry J. Greenham (1929) Ltd* (1969) 4 ITR 226 HC).

Your own witness

Many of the points we have mentioned should be discussed with your own witness prior to the hearing. For example, you should point out that the other side may at times attempt to get an answer that the witness does not want to give or insist on a yes/no when witnesses have a right to give a full explanation.

When your witnesses are being cross-examined, take careful notes on any contradictions, inconsistencies or admissions which might undermine your case, and any statements your witness has made which need to be set in context or given full explanation.

Cross-examination

When your opponent has finished examining the employer's witness, you are entitled to ask him or her questions. This is called cross-examination. It involves inspecting, probing and testing the evidence given in the examination. **It has three major purposes:**

(1) to let the tribunal see which facts are admitted and which are in dispute, by putting **your version of what happened to the witness;**

(2) to **weaken the case** your opponent has established through questions to the witness;

(3) to **establish facts which are favourable to your case**.

In cross-examining you are trying to get the tribunal to think:

- How reliable is this witness?
- Is she or he telling the truth?
- Is the account accurate?
- Has she or he missed anything out?
- There is another side to this witness's story, how does it compare?

Cross-examination should be:

- based on the evidence the witness has given;
- based on the credibility or standing of the witness to give that evidence.

You have a right to cross-examine any witnesses called by your opponent.

■ Joe McBride was not given the chance of cross-examining a witness as the tribunal felt it would be simply a waste of time. They went on to find for the employer. McBride appealed. The court felt that it was doubtful whether the decision would have been any different had he been given the chance to cross-examine. They *felt* that the decision was correct but it was not possible *to say with certainty* that new facts might not emerge under cross-examination. McBride should have been given the chance and a rehearing was ordered (*McBride v British Railways Board* (1972) 7 ITR 84 NIRC).

The chairperson should not interfere with your cross-examination, as long as it is relevant to the case and is not repetitive or unfairly harassing.

■ A chairperson was alleged to have said that he was catching a train leaving Darlington at 5 p.m. At 4 o'clock, when a witness had given her evidence, he said, 'I am going to impose a time limit on the cross-examination of Mrs McTiernan'. Lord Chief Justice Parker said: 'If I was satisfied that the Chairman of this or any other tribunal had arbitrarily imposed a time limit on cross-examination then clearly this court would interfere but I am far from satisfied that this is what happened here' (*Vickers v Hudson Bros* (1970) 5 ITR 259).

You should have prepared, where possible, the general framework of your cross-examination and the substance of important questions *before* the case, although you need to react flexibly to what is actually said. Whilst your opponent is questioning a witness **you should be taking careful notes**. Distinguish evidence which you agree with, and which is useful for your case, from evidence on which you wish to cross-examine, i.e. admissions which might harm your case, contradictions or statements which you think need fuller explanation.

You may wish to use different sheets of paper or different colour pencils or asterisks to do this. If you leave a margin you will be able to job down comments and the kind of questions you want to ask. Keep notes or numbered pages headed for each witness.

Your notes will also be useful in cross-examination if the witness denies she or he said something in the examination in chief. If in cross-examination you say, 'Ms X, I believe that what you said was . . .' and you receive the reply, 'I said no such thing', you should appeal to the chairperson so that the notes can be checked with yours. Notes are essential for cross-examination and also for your summing up.

When you have eliminated and selected, sorted the wheat from the chaff, the next question is, **do you need to cross-examine?** If the witness has said nothing that damages your case it may be best to leave well alone. Harmful points may come out in cross-examination. **Do not feel that cross-examination is a must.** On the other hand, if the witness has stated *disputed facts*, and you do not challenge them, then the tribunal can imply acceptance from your silence.

In a recent and fairly typical case the cross-examination was limited to:

Representative: You mentioned that you let Phillips know exactly what the job involved when you took her on.
Witness: Yes, I spent half an hour going through salary, holiday and pension arrangements and so on. Then I took her round the office and showed her exactly how things worked.
Representative: Did you give her a written contract?
Witness: No.
Representative: Did you give her a written statement of her basic terms and conditions as required by the Employment Protection (Consolidation) Act?
Witness: No.
Representative: Why not?
Witness: I did not think it was required.

The worker's side had no disagreement with what had happened as stated by the employer. It was the legal significance that they were arguing about. There was no point in going through a long cross-examination for the sake of it. However, a telling point was made: the employer was ignorant of and did not live up to legal obligations in one area.

In another case the cross-examination went:

Representative: Just let me clarify one point. Smith had been late back from lunch three times in the last eight months?
Witness: That's correct.
Representative: What about the records of comparable workers on this?
Witness: I don't know. I only asked the supervisor about Smith.
Representative: Why was that?
Witness: Because of his previous poor workmanship.
Representative: But it is possible that others might have been late as frequently.
Witness: I suppose so.

The aim here was to put the witness's original statement in context. It looked different the first time round.

In many tribunal cases cross-examination will simply involve making a few points like this. The long complex struggle seen in other legal arenas and in dramatisations is fairly rare.

Some important points

- **Leading questions can be asked in cross-examination;** sometimes they may minimise the impact of evidence.
- **Be firm with the witness**, but do not bully or browbeat. The representative who gives the impression of a skilled nurse with his or her own witnesses and a bar-room brawler with the other side's witnesses is not going to make a good impression on the tribunal. They will appreciate the pressures a witness is under and, initially at least, will tend to sympathise with the witness against a sarcastic or discourteous representative.
- Always **give the witness a fair chance to answer your question** in the way she or he wishes. If it gradually becomes clear that the witness is being evasive, or is just incapable of answering in a straightforward way, then you are entitled

to insist on a straight answer by repeating the question. But do not always demand yes or no. The explanation may be useful.

You should get out of your mind any images of *The Caine Mutiny* or *The Trials of Oscar Wilde*. You are not (generally) cross-examining a bent copper, nor are you a Perry Mason-type television lawyer ruthlessly dissecting the witness so that the evidence is left without a shred of credibility. Regard yourself as a patient, carefully prepared journeyman, try to pare away points and chisel out doubts and qualifications, so that you limit and modify the value of the evidence.

Highly unlikely

Representative: Ms Jones, you just stated that Ms Smith had never received a written warning.
Witness: Yes, that's right.
Representative: Would you like to study this [passes to witnesses and tribunal copy of final written warning dated a month ago].
Witness: [Stuttering silence.]

More likely

Representative: You said that you knew Jones well?
Witness: Yes.
Representative: How many times have you met her?
Witness: A few times.
Representative: Can you be a little more precise?
Witness: At least once or twice.

- **Stop when you get what you want.** In the last example move on. If you ask for more you get more of what you don't want. The once or twice might be explained further as once or twice since they both worked for the company, but they were both at school together and worked at another company for ten years altogether on the same job and shift. However, if your opponent is alert, she or he may come back to this point in re-examination and try to limit any damage that you have done. Don't try and double your money by getting the same point from another witness. If your questions are too long the witness has time to think.
- **Keep your questioning relevant and short.** Do not go on and on. If you do not hit pay dirt in a reasonable time, cut your

losses. If you keep on probing an unshakeable witness then you will simply be providing a second opportunity to reinforce and firm up his or her story in the tribunal's minds. If the witness gets the chance to repeat the evidence often and convincingly, you yourself may end end up accepting his or her version. Moreover, the chairperson's patience will be taxed by continuing questions when you have reached an impasse.

- If you do gain a point or admission, **do not chortle exultantly**, slap your thigh, start making a speech to the tribunal regarding its importance and then proceed to lecture the witness. Pause to let it sink in and then move on. You can stress its importance in your summing up.
- **Do not try and discredit a witness because of minor contradictions and discrepancies.**

Representative: Could you tell me again what time the conversation occurred?
Witness: Three thirty.
Representative: Mr Smith stated it was quarter to four.
Witness: Well, I'm not sure, I suppose it could have been.
Representative: You're not sure . . . You suppose! Heaven help us! I wonder whether you really remember *anything* that happened that afternoon!

In a situation where nothing much hangs on this minor difference, it is the representative who is likely to make an extremely unfavourable impression on the tribunal.

- **You should be in control of the situation.** After all, you can choose the parts of the evidence to question and the form and substance of the questions themselves. The witness may be uncertain as to how much you know. You are more likely to be adept at speaking and asking relevant questions than the witness, but once more careful preparation before the during the hearing is the key.
- You will often hear experienced lawyers say, **'Never ask a question if you have not a good idea of what the answer will be.'** This is a generalisation which is almost always correct. Do not completely avoid difficult questions, but do approach them very carefully.

In one case a foreman of 15 years' experience with the company had been dismissed for fighting. He had no previous disciplinary record. There were no witnesses as to who had started the fight. One of the jobs of his representative was to establish that it was unlikely, given his background, bearing and behaviour, that he would have been the aggressor. The approach with the witness was straightforward and abrupt: 'Is it likely that he would start a fight?' The representative, who had not done as much detailed research as he should have done, was taken aback by a reply detailing a pub brawl some years before and domestic violence.

It would have been better if he had gradually worked up to the dangerous point on these lines.

Representative: You have known him about eight years?
Witness: About that.
Representative: Is he good at his work?
Witness: Yes, he's a conscientious worker.
Representative: You said he had never been in trouble before.
Witness: Yes, that's right.
Representative: Was he involved in any other activities at work?
Witness: Yes, he was a member of the social club committee and played for the works football team.
Representative: A useful member of the committee?
Witness: Yes, he made an effective contribution.
Representative: Any other social activities?
Witness: No, but he used to regularly attend union meetings.
Representative: So he was involved in the social life of the factory over a number of years?
Witness: Yes.
Representative: And there were never any problems?
Witness: No.
Representative: Was he popular?
Witness: Not particularly. He was regarded more as the steady and sound sort.
Representative: So given all this a fellow worker would have been very surprised if he had assaulted and seriously injured a workmate.
Witness: I suppose so.

This approach will not always work, but a cautious build-up concealing the objective gives you a better chance. To ask directly involves a greater risk. Again, in this example, it might be as well to let matters rest there. If you try to get a stronger 'character reference', you may forfeit the gains that you have already made.

- Many experienced advocates point out that **the last question** you ask and, hopefully, its answer should crown the objective of your line of questioning and distil the impression that you have been trying to create.

Representative: Have you ever heard of the ACAS Code of Practice on how to deal fairly with workers in a dismissal situation?
Witness: No.

Some techniques of cross-examination

It is no good just going over and over the evidence the witness has given in the same way, hoping he or she will magically change it, under your persistent questioning. This will actually make the evidence appear stronger and more convincing. You can try several varied approaches depending on the case.

(1) The head-on collision
This can be used in the rare situation where you are in a position to destroy or severely weaken the employer's case. You can only use this where you are able to confront the witness with facts she or he cannot deny.

For example: a worker is claiming a redundancy payment and you have an internal memo which shows there is no intention to replace the worker, although the employers have stated that they are still trying to fill the job; or a worker is claiming victimisation for trade union activities, and you produce a blacklist from the employers' association. These are for most of us once in a lifetime situations.

(2) Undermining the witness
In one famous court case, Sir Norman Birkett cross-examined an expert engineer and fire assessor, who claimed for the defence that a fire had been accidentally caused. This evidence coming from an expert would have a powerful impact.

Birkett: What is the coefficient of the expansion of brass?
Witness: I'm afraid I cannot answer that question off hand.
Birkett: If you do not know, say so. What do I mean by the term?

Witness: You want to know what is the expansion of the metal under heat.

Birkett: I asked you what is the coefficient of the expansion of brass. Do you know?

Witness: Put that way probably I do not.

Birkett: You are an engineer?

Witness: I dare say I am.

(3) The lancet

If you have no external material with which to contradict the witness's story, you have to probe internally into that story to tease out its weaknesses. Many statements may be made which have no foundation: 'She or he was always in trouble with the foreman'; 'She or he was often late', 'She or he spent too much time on union business'. Always examine the foundations and assumptions of these kind of statements.

If a witness vividly remembers a central point, does she or he remember other details of the situation? If you can, by probing, show that their witness does not, then it may lead the tribunal to question *why* he or she should remember that one significant detail.

If you feel a witness is not telling the truth, a deluge of rapid short sharp questions on all details of the situation may tax his or her powers of invention.

Sometimes a bit of good thinking may limit the use of a witness's evidence:

Representative: You said he was half an hour late on three occasions that week.

Witness: Yes, he came in at about nine o'clock.

Representative: What time do you start work?

Witness: Nine thirty.

Sometimes this technique can be immensely successful. In one well-known case where a taxi driver stated categorically that he was driving quite slowly, the barrister, through careful detailed probing, gradually got him to admit that he had skidded, mounted the pavement, smashed a plate-glass window, knocked over several stalls, three people and a lamp post – details rather inconsistent with 'driving quite slowly'!

(4) Insinuation

A mixture of probing and insinuation is probably the most common method you will use. You are trying to build up a different version of what the witness has said in examination by bringing out new facts or interpretations. An example of insinuation is on page 196.

Questions from the tribunal

The tribunal can ask the witness questions at any stage. They will normally do this *after* cross-examination. They may ask questions simply because they do not understand particular details or explanations, or because they see contradictions or inconsistencies, or do not find the story credible. A witness who has escaped unscathed from cross-examination may still be pinned down at this stage by the tribunal, who have had the benefit of listening to the examination and cross-examination as 'outsiders'.

Putting your case

One of the rules of evidence connected with cross-examination is that you have to put your version of what happened to your opponents' witnesses. Where any of the facts of the case are disputed, you have to raise them so that the witness has the chance to deal with them. At times it can be difficult to canvass *all* points in dispute. Think about this before the case, jot down a checklist while your opponent examines his or her witnesses.

The 1980 Regulations

Reference to cross-examination is omitted from these rules, which only refer to the right to 'question' witnesses called by your opponent, subject to the tribunal conducting the hearing in the way 'it considers most suitable to the clarification issues before it'. This is intended to create more informality, but your aims and the general conduct of this stage will be the same as those involved in the cross-examination process.

However, the changes encourage more intervention from the tribunal and give them more control over the process. If the tribunal interrupt you with their own questions, let them have their say. But if they interfere with what you are trying to do, patiently explain your purpose and method in pursuing a particular line of questioning. Do not be put off your stride by interruptions from your opponent. Explain why you are dealing with the witness in this way. If you are firm but polite the chair will usually allow you to continue.

Problems with the chair

The same goes if you wish to interrupt to make a protest. If you feel that the tribunal is dealing with you so unreasonably as to affect the success of your case by, for example, interfering with your examination, then you can make a formal application for the matter to be noted on the record of the case or ultimately ask for a new chair. Do not do this on the basis of minor incidents. Do so only if you feel your case is in danger. If you do raise the matter, do so calmly, pointing at *specific criticisms* rather than complaining about 'general attitude'. Above all, **do not just walk out – this may simply mean you lose your case** (see *John Laing Services Ltd v Wellstead* (1982) EAT 160/82). If you need to consider the matter, adjourn.

■ Mortimer took a constructive dismissal case to a tribunal. The chair breezily introduced the case with the comment 'Why are we here today, because you obviously resigned?', interrupted his cross-examination and pushed him to finish. Mortimer appealed successfully to the EAT on the grounds that, all in all, he did not have a fair hearing and the case was sent back to a different tribunal to be reheard (*Mortimer v Reading Windows Ltd* (1977) ICR 511 EAT) (see also Chapter 13).

There may also be a material irregularity where the tribunal discusses the case with one side but not the other (*Todd v Susan Small* (1982) EAT 30/82).

Re-examination

Next, you are entitled to re-examine your witness. You cannot bring up new matters here. The purpose is to deal with problems that have come out of the cross-examination, not to bring in points you forgot about in examination, unless they have emerged in cross-examination. However, if you *have* left vital evidence out, you should explain this to the chair and ask for it to be allowed in the interest of achieving a fair result.

The aim is to explain misunderstandings, qualify admissions and put particular answers into context and perspective. **You may not need to re-examine if you are satisfied with the way things have gone.** Don't do it simply because the opportunity is there. Even at this late stage you could upset the applicant. Is there anything *important* or *damaging* which has come out of cross-examination which you need to cut down to size?

In the ordinary courts you would not be entitled to ask leading questions in re-examining your own witness. You can do so here but again, the impact will be lessened if your witness now agrees with you in responding to leading questions, after having disagreed under the probing of your opponent. A series of leading questions is the least effective method. What you will normally be attempting to do here is to insinuate facts or interpretations which place a different complexion on the answers given in cross-examination.

> *Representative:* You just agreed that it was against the works' rules.
> *Witness:* Yes.
> *Representative:* Why did you do it?
> *Witness:* Everybody did it.
> *Representative:* Everybody?
> *Witness:* Over the last year everybody on my section at one time or another.
> *Representative:* And the supervisor?
> *Witness:* She knew it went on and accepted it.

Occasionally you may try to draw the sting from a pretty devastating attack on the credibility of your witness.

> *Representative:* Are you a particular friend of Ms Smith?
> *Witness:* No.
> *Representative:* Is there any reason then why you should not be frank with the tribunal?
> *Witness:* None at all.

Remember: If a witness has to leave after giving evidence, ask the tribunal for permission.

If a witness is being cross-examined when the tribunal adjourns, he or she must not discuss the case with his or her own side's representative during the interval.

No case to answer

You have listened to the employer's evidence, and it is preposterous. You get up and say: 'The burden of proof is on the employer. He has failed to discharge it. There is no point wasting further time. It should be clear now that there is no case to answer.' What is the tribunal likely to do if you (or your opponent, if you have gone first) argue that the case should be stopped on the grounds that the evidence has failed to prove the case?

This problem has generally come up with constructive dismissal and discrimination cases, although it can apply to all situations.

At first the EAT seemed to rule against this kind of submission being accepted. 'The duty of a tribunal is to hear evidence on both sides' (*Buskin v Vacutech* (1977) 12 ITR 107 EAT). This was taken in tribunals to mean that there was 'an inflexible rule of law and practice that in all cases . . . a tribunal is bound whatever the circumstances to hear the respondent's evidence'. But in another case the EAT expressly said that this was not the principle of the Buskin case:

> the ordinary general practice should be to hear what has to be said on both sides. Our experience shows that where this is not done confusion often arises and even if it does not a feeling of injustice is left with one party or the other. But that passage was not intended to say nor do we intend to say that there are no exceptions at all. Cases may be put forward which are so obviously hopeless that it would be a waste of time to call on the respondents to call evidence and this prolongs the proceedings . . . So yes, there may be exceptional cases but ordinarily it is better to hear what everybody has to say (*Ridley v GEC Machines* (1978) 13 ITR 195 EAT; *Lothian Health Board v Johnstone* (1981) IRLR 321 EAT).

The basic objection to 'no case to answer' has been stressed in other cases.

> The general approach must be that in cases concerned with dismissal, whether it be constructive or direct dismissal, the concept of 'no case to answer' is somewhat out of place . . . there is a danger in such a case of not giving a fair solution to the problem (*Walker v Josiah Wedgwood & Sons Ltd* (1978) ICR 744 EAT).

Some tribunals do allow the 'no case to answer' in what they regard as exceptional cases.

■ Mrs Hill had been certified as unfit to work on 'wet' machines. She claimed the foreman ordered her to do some wet work, there was an argument and she was sent home. She was then off sick. But when she came back it was on the basis that she would do dry jobs only. On the day she returned the foreman refused to let her go on fire practice which involved extra money; there was an argument in which she swore at him. She was later allowed to do fire practice but resigned, as she found it impossible to work in the atmosphere created by certain employees, and claimed constructive dismissal. At the end of her evidence the employers submitted that there was no case to answer as the employers had not on her evidence committed fundamental breaches of contract which entitled her to resign. The tribunal agreed on the grounds that there was no connection between her being sent home and the second incident which anyway was not a breach of a fundamental term of contract (*Hill v Rearsby Components* (1979) COIT 921/165).

- **If you argue 'no case to answer'** you do not stand or fall by this argument. You are still entitled to present your own evidence if the tribunal reject your submission (*Walker v Josiah Wedgwood*).
- You should only **use this submission in exceptional circumstances**, where it is clear that the employer has not a leg to stand on. You will have to *justify* your submission and in most cases the easiest way of doing so is by presenting your own evidence.
- Particularly **in constructive dismissal cases**, be on guard against the employer making a submission and ask for the right to argue against it.

Closing the case

You should generally make a brief **closing statement**. Refresh the tribunal's memory and put the essence of the argument just before they adjourn to decide. If you need to marshal your arguments, ask for a brief adjournment.

- **Briefly outline the salient facts;** not all the evidence that you have given, but the crucial ingredients. If there is a conflict of fact, argue why your evidence should be preferred. Point out omissions or inconsistencies in your opponent's case.
- **Put your general arguments** as to why these facts should make you the winner. Stress your own strong points and dissect your opponent's arguments and answer points made against you.

- **Present your legal arguments**, mentioning any cases and explaining why the tribunal should follow them.
- **If your opponent has used any legal arguments** or precedents, explain why they are unapplicable. If you summed up first, you will have a final right to address the tribunal on any legal points your opponent has raised. As you will generally sum up first, you should consider using this final opportunity.

11.

Costs

In an ordinary court one side may have to pay some of the costs or legal expenses of the other party. One of the things you have to keep in mind from beginning to end of your case, is whether you might end up having to pay some or all of your opponent's costs. You need to look at this chapter before you decide whether to bring a case and to look at some of the pitfalls that you may fall into, in the preparation and conduct of your case, which can lead to the tribunal awarding costs against you. Costs can, of course, be awarded in your favour against your opponent, so look at these rules to see if you think that the employer should be penalised if his or her behaviour causes *you* problems.

Where to find the law
Industrial Tribunals Regulations 12.

Costs in tribunals

When tribunals were established there was concern that workers might be put off bringing cases if large costs could be awarded against them. Special rules therefore apply to tribunals, which should not *normally* award costs. **Costs may be awarded:**

- where **either party has acted frivolously or vexatiously or otherwise unreasonably**; or
- where the tribunal has postponed or adjourned the hearing, against the person the tribunal feels has caused the delay, **whether or not that party has acted frivolously or vexatiously**.

   This applies where an employer: (a) in an unfair dismissal case, has been informed at least seven days before the hearing that the worker wants his or her job back; or (b) has failed to allow a woman to return to work under maternity leave provisions of the EP(C)A. Then if the employer has to ask for an adjournment because he or she is not able to show reasonable evidence as to why the worker should not be reinstated or re-engaged, the tribunal **must** award costs against the employer unless he or she can show a special reason.

The tribunal can order either side to pay:

- the other side a sum of money specified by the tribunal.
- the other side a sum of money to be 'taxed', i.e. decided upon by the County Court, on the scales used in the County Court (see below).
- back to the Secretary of State for Employment part or the whole of any expenses or allowances they have received for attending the tribunal.

The County Court operates four scales of costs:

Lower scale	£26–£100
Scale 1	£100–£500
Scale 2	£501–£3,000
Scale 3	Exceeding £3,000

If the tribunal orders costs to be 'taxed', it will stipulate the scale within which costs must lie. Costs include legal fees and other expenses involved in relation to the case. The EAT has recently said that the scale chosen by tribunals should reflect the **amount of work** involved for the party in the case **not the financial importance** of the case in terms of compensation (*Field v Brush Electrical Machines Ltd* (1979) EAT 321/79).

In one case Kilner Brown J. commented that:

the Employment Appeal Tribunal finds itself extremely embarrassed because there is no power in suitable cases to award costs out of central funds. It may well be that if this is said often enough and long enough ultimately somebody will take notice of it and make sure that the regulations are altered so that in certain proper cases an award of costs can be made out of central funds (*Hill v Sabco Houseward (UK) Ltd* (1977) ICR 888 EAT).

Frivolous and vexatious

As defined in the *Shorter Oxford Dictionary*, the word 'frivolous' means manifestly futile, characterised by lack of seriousness, sense or reverence given to trifling, silly . . . the word 'vexatious' means instituted without sufficient grounds for the purpose of causing trouble or annoyance (*Durrant v Baker Oil Tools UK Ltd* (1974) IRLR 290).

If the employee knows that there is no substance in his claim and that it is bound to fail or if the claim is on the face of it so manifestly misconceived that it can have no prospect of success it may be deemed frivolous and an abuse of the procedure of the tribunal to pursue it. If an employee brings a hopeless claim not with any expectation of recovering compensation but out of spite to harrass his employers or for some other improper motive he acts vexatiously and likewise abuses the procedure (*E. T. Marler Ltd v Robertson* (1974) ICR 72 NIRC).

The implication in this statement and in other cases is that action can be 'frivolous' where the tribunal objectively decides that the case is 'meritless', or where a party knows subjectively that the case is a bad one. In early cases the tendency was more to award costs here in 'bad faith' cases, where the party's attitude is under scrutiny. The approach has become tougher: regardless of the attitude of the party, should the case have been brought at all, given the legal position?

Remember that either party can be frivolous and vexatious, and not just in bringing or defending a case but at any stage of the proceedings.

■ Mrs Laws was dismissed because she was found to have been paying members of staff for overtime with food rather than cash. She was sacked without notice and without a chance to offer any explanation. The company threatened her with a legal case for damages if she took legal advice. At the tribunal hearing, where she was represented by a barrister, the employers failed to call any evidence, so she asked for costs. The EAT upheld the tribunal decision that costs should be awarded. They felt that the correct grounds were, however, frivolity and not vexatious behaviour. The latter suggests 'some spite or desire to harass the other side to the legislation or the existence of some other improper motive'. Whilst there was some evidence for this they preferred to find frivolity. '. . . they had never investigated the case at all or given Mrs Laws the chance to be heard. Secondly, they behaved in a way and made allegations of a character which made it inevitable that she would regard the proceeding with great seriousness resulting in her instructing solicitors and counsel. And thirdly, the realisation that the case was hopeless could well have dawned on them earlier' (*Cartiers Superfoods Ltd v Laws* (1978) IRLR 315 EAT).

Otherwise unreasonable

In addition to awarding costs where a party's behaviour has been frivolous or vexatious, the 1980 regulations now give tribunals the power to award costs where a party's conduct has been 'otherwise unreasonable'. This will avoid some of the technicality surrounding 'frivolous' and 'vexatious' and make it easier for a tribunal to award costs. It should be read in relation also to the new powers of pre-hearing assessment (see pages 92 and 93).

Costs and the union

The money will be to reimburse the other side for their legal expenses. The Litigants in Person (Costs and Expenses) Act 1975, which allows lay people to claim their costs in preparing and presenting a case, has not been extended to tribunals although it has been to the EAT. Only *parties* to the case can recover costs, so it would have to be the member, not the union, who did so.

■ The CRE applied for costs on the grounds that Walsall Metropolitan Borough Council had unreasonably delayed withdrawing their appeal against a tribunal decision that they had unlawfully discriminated against Ms Sidhu. This had caused the CRE to incur costs and expenses on her behalf through the council's fault. The EAT agreed but said the rules only allowed them to award costs to parties. Ms Sidhu had not incurred costs or expenses as she was under no obligation to repay the CRE for any expense. The council should have to pay costs but were able to get off scot-free (*Walsall Metropolitan Borough Council v Sidhu* (1979) ICR 519 EAT).

As unions are in the same position as the CRE, they would not be able to recover from the employer. The 1980 Regulations specifically refer to 'costs and *expenses*' so that this should mean that either side could include non-legal representation and advice.

What about the position where the employers try to get costs against the union?

■ Ms Carr lost her unfair dismissal case. She was represented by the GMWU regional organiser. The employer asked for and was awarded costs on the grounds that the claim was frivolous and vexatious. The tribunal awarded the costs not against Ms Carr but against the union taking its full resources into account as if it were a County Court case. They also refused to allow the official an adjournment to take legal advice on this situation. The EAT said that they were wrong. The practice in the tribunals of awarding small sums against individuals in exceptional cases rather than the larger costs awarded on court scales was reasonable given applicants' limited resources. Moreover the orders for costs should not have been made against the union (*Carr v Allen Bradley Electronics* (1980) IRLR 263 EAT).

However, the EAT left this position open for the future. They said:

There may be cases where the role of the union in pursuing the litigation and the union's knowledge or means of knowledge of the lack of merit in the claim may make it appropriate to take account of the union's position in deciding the order for costs. In such circumstances it may be that the union will indemnify the claimant in respect of the costs even though the order itself will be against the claimant. *We do not wish to say anything that may fetter the exercise by a tribunal of its discretion in future hypothetical cases* [emphasis added].

In other words, in some cases where the official has been thoroughly involved and should have known that the case was frivolous or vexatious, it may be right to take the union's financial position into account when deciding how much to award. Although the costs would be against the member, the union might feel pressure to pay the costs although many unions warn members at the outset that the problem of costs is *their* responsibility.

Examples of costs

In the early days, tribunals were reluctant to award costs as the law was new and they did not wish to frighten people off. However, recently more and more awards of costs are being made and the amounts tend to drift upwards. You will not normally get the whole of your costs from the defaulting party. The normal award is a specific sum, say between £40 and £100 which appears reasonable to the tribunal. Taxed costs, however, are on the increase and the sum is likely to be nearer £500. In *Kalibala v Senate of the Inns of Court* (1979) EAT 748/78, the EAT reduced an award against one respondent to £300 but upheld an award against another of £500. Costs will be assessed on the basis of the *expenses* the winner has *actually incurred*, the *ability* of the loser to pay, and the *degree of gravity* of his misconduct.

(1) Non-appearance

■ Mrs Harvey made no appearance at the hearing which was adjourned to another date. She failed to turn up then, the tribunal went ahead, found that there was no dismissal, and ordered her to pay costs of £10 because her failure to attend without informing anyone concerned had caused unnecessary expense and inconvenience in setting up the second hearing (*Harvey v Yankee Traveller Restaurant* (1976) IRLR 35).

■ Yates was arrested for stealing one of his employer's carpets. He denied he was guilty but pleaded guilty at the trial, did not reply to the tribunal's letter asking if he wished to go on, and failed to turn up at the hearing. He was found to have been acting frivolously and vexatiously and ordered to pay £50 to the Secretary of State for wasting public funds (*Yates v Cavalier Carpets* (1979) COIT 932/24).

(2) Late withdrawal

■ Cudd's case, already postponed because of problems over further particulars, was set for 17 October. That day at 8.20 a.m. he phoned to withdraw. The employer's brief and witnesses were informed on arrival. His withdrawal was frivolous and vexatious given that he had, on the face of it, little prospect of success and the employer had heavy costs. Cudd had to pay on County Court Scale 4 (*Cudd v Kennel Club* (1978) COIT 818/218).

(3) Further particulars

■ McMaster was ordered to give further particulars on 18 August. He did nothing despite being asked again on 6 September. His application was struck out. In view of his poor financial position costs were *not* awarded against him although his conduct *was* frivolous and vexatious but he was not given any expenses (*McMaster v Airport Private Hotel* (1978) COIT 805/81).

(4) Ulterior motive

■ Patel was injured at work and sacked. He was involved in negotiations for compensation for his injury and also brought a case for unfair dismissal. The hearing was adjourned three times and eventually called off on the settlement of his compensation claim. The employers were awarded costs. His case was 'something subsidiary to the claim in respect of industrial injury. It was used as a bargaining factor rather than a substantive claim on its own merits . . . such manoeuvring amounts to an abuse of the process' (*Patel v Steams Laboratories* (1978) COIT 738/159).

(5) Calling witnesses

■ Jack Llewellyn's dismissal for a clocking offence was found to have been fair. He called as witnesses 14 other workers 'many of them under the compulsion of a witness order. We have no hesitation in finding that his conduct has been frivolous with knowledge of the demerits of his case and with the intention of deceiving the tribunal . . . it may well have also been vexatious as being intended deliberately to annoy the respondents . . .' (*Llewellyn v British Steel Llanwern* (1972) COIT 8036/72).

(6) Threatening witnesses

■ Harry Francis was taking a claim of unfair dismissal. During the week of the hearing he visited his former workplace and threatened witnesses. In fact he won his case but had to pay £100 costs for vexatious behaviour (*Francis v Trotkarn Ltd* (1979) COIT 928/227).

(7) Political platform

■ Gerry Healy claimed that after his dismissal he had been blacklisted by the Employers Federation and that to get rid of him, the site management had made a special payment to his employer to leave the site and pay off his 25 workers. The tribunal said that Healy had simply wished to air a grievance for which there was 'not a shred of evidence'. This was frivolous and he had to pay £150 towards his employer's costs (*Healy v South Humberside Insulation Co.* (1978) COIT 871/221).

(8) Adjournments

- The employer's representative handed 66 documents, 45 minutes before the hearing, to Hickey's representative, who asked for an adjournment in order to read and digest them. The tribunal granted this and ordered the employer to pay £150 costs. The employer appealed on the grounds that his behaviour was not frivolous or vexatious. The decision was upheld. There is no frivolous or vexatious restriction in relation to costs of an adjournment or postponement (*Ladbroke Racing v Hickey* (1979) IRLR 273 EAT).

- Rajguru's employer replied to the question 'What was the reason for dismissal?' by stating: 'The employee was spoiling the food and using bad language'.

  At the hearing his representative claimed that the true reason for the dismissal was not apparent. The employer then made five allegations, including 'that the employee smoked during meals' and that he was guilty of bad timekeeping. The worker's side asked for an adjournment to consider these new points, particularly given language difficulties with Rajguru. The tribunal awarded costs against him on the grounds that he should have asked for further particulars before the hearing. The decision was overruled by the EAT. If he *should* have asked for further particulars prior to the hearing, then an adjournment should not have been granted but this was not relevant to the question of whether costs should be awarded (*Rajguru v Top Order Ltd* (1977) ICR 565 EAT).

  - If you keep your head and follow the procedural points we have discussed before and during the tribunal, you should be able to safely navigate the rapids of costs.
  - You must pay some attention to this matter as awards are growing and costs can be large, if the tribunal feels you have messed them about. In a recent case one applicant was ordered to pay his ex-employers £5,000 as his application was a frivolous one. However, the tribunal should normally warn you that you are sailing into troubled waters (*Wrenhurst v Catholic Herald* (1981) EAT 312/81).

- If you feel that the employer's conduct justifies an award to you of costs, ask the tribunal *at the end* of the case, or *at the time* if a postponement or adjournment is being requested. Where one party applied for costs after a case had finished and was awarded £500 the EAT said:

  It might well be a ground for refusing an order for costs that it is made at a very late stage . . . but we find it quite impossible to say that an application must be made during the course of the hearing itself . . . we do not think it would be right to say that there must be an application within 14 days of the entry on the register by analogy to the position when a review is sought (*Zakia v Home Office* (1979) EAT 28/79; *Lothian Health Board v Johnstone* (1981) IRLR 321 EAT).

- If you do not turn up for the hearing and costs are awarded against you then, as long as they are justified, you cannot argue on procedural grounds that you should have been given notice of the costs application (*Rocha v Commonwealth Holiday Inns of Canada Ltd* (1980) EAT 13/80).

- If in trouble, remember to quote to the tribunal the statement of the NIRC: 'Ordinary experience of life frequently teaches us that that which is plain for all to see once the dust of battle has subsided was far from clear to the combatants when they took up arms' (*E. T. Marler Ltd v Robertson* (1974) ICR 72 NIRC).

Expenses and allowances

Allowances may be paid to the parties to defray their expenses in attending a tribunal hearing. Allowances can be paid to witnesses, unless the tribunal feels that they were not reasonably justified, and also to representatives. However, expenses will not be paid to representatives who are full-time officials of a trade union, or an Employers' Association, or a barrister or a solicitor.

The **cost of travelling** can be paid where public transport is used, if the place of hearing is more than six miles from your home or place of work. The cost is limited to second-class rail fare. If a car is used then there is a mileage allowance.

A **subsistance allowance** is based on a scale which calculates hours of absence from home, with extra if there is an unavoidable

Allowances for attendance at a tribunal

The following allowances may be paid to you, your witnesses and any person representing you (except full-time officials of a workers' or employers' organization, a barrister or a solicitor or other paid representative). Allowances may be refused if the tribunal decides that they were not reasonably justified.

Cost of travelling*

Cost of travelling by public transport, limited to second class by rail, may be paid if the hearing takes place more than six miles from home or place of work. People travelling from overseas including the Channel Islands, Northern Ireland, Eire or the Isle of Man will be paid fares only from the place of arrival in Great Britain.

If a motor vehicle is used, the public transport rate of mileage allowance may be paid, plus 2p a mile for the first passenger carried and 1p a mile for each additional passenger. The rates are based on cubic capacity and are as follows.

	rate per mile
Motor vehicles 251 cc and over	12.7p
151–250 cc	8.6p
150 cc and less	6.4p

Subsistence allowances*

Period of absence from home:	amount
Less than 2½ hours	nil
2½–5 hours	0.88p
5 hours 1 minute–10 hours	£1.75
10 hours 1 minute or more	£4.20

Allowances for an unavoidable night's absence £25.95 or, if the tribunal is held within five miles' radius of Charing Cross, London £32.65.

Loss of earnings (or National Insurance benefit lost which would otherwise be payable)*

Any earnings which are actually lost through absence from work may be repaid up to £19.00 a day – this also applies to the self-employed. Where the performance of remunerative work is merely postponed, no compensation is payable.

Claims

You should apply to the tribunal clerk after the hearing for a form of application if you want to claim any of these allowances.

Form IT114

night's absence. You can also be compensated for **loss of earnings**, which are actually lost through absence from work up to a set figure per day.

If you want to know more about the details of these allowances, you should get a copy of the leaflet, *Industrial Tribunals Procedure (ITL1)*.

At the end of the hearing an expenses form (IT114, see page 209) should be completed and handed to the clerk putting on your case. Where costs are awarded against a party then no expenses are paid to that party and they may be ordered by the tribunal to repay all or part of their allowances to the Department of Employment. The party which wins the case should *not* be paid both costs and allowances in respect of the same expenses.

12.

Bringing home the bacon

If you win your case you may get grits or you may get gravy – depending on the preparation you have done and the skill with which you present your arguments. Far too many representatives, having won the case, understandably breathe a sigh of relief and place themselves in the hands of the tribunal as far as the gelt goes. **This means that all too often it does not go very far and that many members get less than they deserve.** As with all else – **never rely on the tribunal**.

There is a body of rules governing tribunal awards and if you know them you can use them. You will see that like all legal rules they are broad and leave a lot of discretion to the tribunal. Whether that discretion is exercised generously or parsimoniously will depend on how you raise the law, the arguments and the evidence. In this chapter we discuss some of the problems involved in getting the remedy you want.

Remember: You will want to look at this chapter in detail when you are preparing your case and *well before* the hearing.
Where to find the law
Industrial Tribunals Regulations 9
EP(C)A ss. 24, 26, 68–76, 81–102 sch. 4, 7, 13, 14.
EA 80 s. 9.
EA 82 ss. 2–9.

Tribunal remedies

Tribunal remedies take three forms:

- **A declaration of rights.** This can be made, for example, under the Equal Pay or Sex Discrimination Acts, but is not legally enforceable. A declaration under the Employment Act, however, in favour of a worker unreasonably expelled or refused admission to a union, can be later enforced by a compensation award.

- **An order of reinstatement or re-engagement.** This will be relevant in unfair dismissal cases, although of course failure to comply is merely visited by a compensation award.
- **Award of compensation.** This is generally what you end up with in most tribunal cases if you win.

In different cases you will be asking for compensation on slightly different lines. For example, in Equal Pay cases you may be asking for up to six months' back pay. In a time-off case you want compensation for any money lost, and for compensation to punish the employer for his or her behaviour. **You should carefully check the specific remedies for the particular case that you are bringing.** We look in detail at the remedies for unfair dismissal, which produces most cases.

Reinstatement and re-engagement

If the tribunal decides a worker has been unfairly dismissed, they must explain what orders of reinstatement and re-engagement can be made and ask if the worker wants the tribunal to make an order. (As far as you are concerned, that *should* have been settled long ago.) If the worker does *not*, that is that, and the tribunal moves on to compensation.

- **A reinstatement order** is intended to return the worker to the orginal job and to reimburse any loss, as if he or she had not been sacked in the first place.
- Where this is not practicable, a **re-engagement order** obliges the employer or an associated employer to take the worker on in a job 'comparable to that from which he was dismissed or other suitable employment'. The terms of a re-engagement recommendation are in the tribunal's discretion. They should 'so far as is reasonably practicable' be as favourable as a reinstatement recommendation.

Should an order be made?

This is the first question for the tribunal. They should *first* consider reinstatement and *only* then re-engagement. In deciding whether an order for reinstatement or re-engagement should be made, the tribunal should consider the wishes of the worker; the practicability of the employer abiding by the order; and whether the worker caused or contributed to the dismissal.

Assuming the worker does want the job back, the tribunal

must decide if it is *practicable*. As a general rule a tribunal should not take into account the fact that a dismissed worker has been permanently replaced, when considering whether it is *practicable* for the employer to comply with an order, *unless* the employer shows:

- it was **not practicable** to arrange for the dismissed worker's job to be done without taking on a permanent replacement; or
- the replacement was engaged after the lapse of **a reasonable period** without having been informed that the sacked worker wanted the job back;
- and that **in both these cases**, when the employer took on the replacement it was **no longer reasonable** to arrange for the sacked worker's job to be done except by a permanent replacement.

That is why it is important to stress once more the necessity of including reinstatement/re-engagement on the application form. You should also have details of the job, surrounding work situation, and state of employer's business from relevant shop stewards, to combat any arguments the employer raises about the necessity of filling the job with a permanent replacement.

The tribunal look not only at the ability of the employer to provide a job. *Practicable* is not the same as *possible*. '. . . the tribunal ought to consider the consequences of re-engagement in the industrial relations scene in which it will take place' (*Coleman v Magnet Joinery Ltd* (1973) IRLR 361; *British Aerospace v Mafe* (1980) EAT 565/80).

Generally therefore, no orders will be made in a closed shop situation (*Sarvent v Central Electricity Generating Board* (1976) IRLR 66), unless there are special circumstances (*Goodbody v British Railways Board* (1977) IRLR 84), where there are likely to be problems with management or other workers (*Thornton v S. J. Kitchin Ltd* (1972) IRLR 46; *James v Bainbridge Highland Garage* (1972) IRLR 52), or where the worker was incompetent or suffered from illness (*Oliso-Emosingoit v Inner London Magistrates Court Service* (1977) EAT 139/77; *McCauley v Cementation Chemicals Ltd* (1972) IRLR 71). On the other hand, the tribunal can look at the possibility of a comparable job (*Todd v North Eastern Electricity Board* (1975) IRLR 130) or the possibility of re-engagement at a future date when an illness has been cured (*Newlands v J. Howard & Co. Ltd* (1973) IRLR 9).

Be prepared to take on and undermine the employer's arguments as to why an order should not be made:

■ A woman was sacked after numerous absences, the last being on account of pregnancy and a miscarriage. The employer claimed that a reinstatement order was not practicable even though he had a vacancy. He relied on 'the long history of the matter . . . the effect of reinstatement on other employees . . . the undermining of management's authority'. The tribunal made an order for reinstatement. They accepted the argument that the absences were for genuine medical reasons, that the company's fears were exaggerated and could be overcome with goodwill, and indeed it was 'part of the duty of good and competent management' to overcome any problems (*George v Beecham Group* (1977) IRLR 43).

Even where the worker has *contributed* to the dismissal, the tribunal can still make an order although they may, for example, make no compensation for loss of wages since the dismissal (*Jones v London Co-operative Society Ltd* (1975) IRLR 110).

The worker refuses the order

If the tribunal do decide to make an order of reinstatement or re-engagement, **ensure that it is as favourable as possible**. You should place your evidence as to the employer's present situation with the aim of returning the worker **as near as is humanly possible to his or her previous position**. The orders will state the dates by which they should be complied with and details of the lost wages and other benefits that the employer must make good.

■ Mrs Hackwood asked for her job back. The tribunal recommended re-engagement on terms less favourable than those in her previous job. The employer accepted the recommendation but she refused it, as the job she had got since leaving was not as well paid but offered better prospects. The tribunal held that her refusal was not unreasonable (*Hackwood v Seal Marine* (1973) IRLR 17).

■ Hallam refused re-engagement initially as a sheet metal worker at the same wages that he had earned as a heating engineer/sheet metal worker with the expectation that he would be given his old job back after a period. He refused the offer and his compensation was reduced by 40 per cent because of this (*Hallam v A. Baguley & Co. Ltd* (1973) COIT 335/73).

If an offer is made by the employer in accordance with a tribunal recommendation and a worker unreasonably refuses it, then the tribunal see that as a failure to minimise the overall loss caused by the dismissal **and reduce cash compensation**. You must consider this point in deciding whether to accept a recommendation. By and large if you have come this far and asked for a recommendation, **you must stick to your guns.**

The employer refuses the order

(a) The employer may not comply *fully* with the details of the order;

(b) the employer may not comply *at all* with the order.

In the first case the tribunal must order the employer to pay the worker an amount it thinks fit 'having regard to the loss sustained by the complainant in consequence of the failure to comply fully with the terms of the order'.

In the second case, before going on to make awards under the two other heads of compensation, the tribunal must make an *additional award* of compensation, unless the employer can satisfy the tribunal that it was not practicable to comply with the recommendation.

The first point to note is that the additional award is a specific sum awarded simply because an order was made and not complied with. It does not affect your other rights to compensation. The second point is that the employer is given two bites at the same cherry: the tribunal has to decide whether reinstatement or re-engagement is practicable as part of the decision as to whether an order should be made and then, having decided it is practicable, they have to look at the situation a second time in deciding whether the employer should be penalised for not carrying out a recommendation that the tribunal has already decided it is practicable to carry out.

This is another example of the law's pains to ensure the maintainance of the employer's prerogative to hire and fire. However, it is extremely unlikely that an employer will be able to show that reinstatement/re-engagement has become impracticable since the tribunal decided that it was practicable. **You should strongly resist any attempt by the employer to do so**, stressing that the onus of proof is on the employer, who should produce detailed evidence as to how and why the situation has changed. You should produce evidence and witnesses from union representatives at the workplace.

Where the employer claims that it is impracticable to comply with a recommendation because a permanent replacement has been engaged, the tribunal must ignore the claim unless the employer can show that it was not practicable to have the job done without engaging a permanent replacement – for example, by a temporary worker. Again, it will be very difficult for the employer to show that this becomes so in the period between a tribunal recommendation being made and the date that it is to become operative where the employer fails to comply with an order.

- If the dismissal was unfair because it involved trade-union activities or racial or sex discrimination, the additional award must be between 26 and 52 weeks' pay.
- If the case involves mainstream unfair dismissal, then the award must not be less than 13 and not more than 26 weeks' pay.
- If the employer fails to *fully* comply the tribunal can make an award of up to £7,500.

The *exact* amount in all three cases is at the discretion of the tribunal. The maximum amount of a week's pay is £140. So the *maximum* additional awards under the two heads will be 52 × £140 = £7,280, 26 × £140 = £3,640. **Remember**, the aim is to penalise the employer for failure to reinstate, not to compensate the worker for loss. You should, therefore, argue that the loss of the job itself is the most important factor for a worker who has asked for reinstatement, and that an employer who rejects a recommendation should be educated by an award in the higher part of the scale.

- In the *George v Beecham Group* case when the company failed to accept the recommendation, the tribunal stated that they were not bound by considerations of what additional loss Ms George would suffer as a result of the company's failure to take her back and that while they felt that this additional loss would be less than 13 weeks they gave her 20 weeks' additional award to show their strong disapproval of the company's decision not to reinstate her (see above).

Basic award

Where no order is made or where it is not carried out, you are entitled to a basic award. The idea here is that every worker who has been sacked should have the equivalent of the statutory redundancy payment to which she or he is entitled. The tribunal will work out the proper award.

(1) They start from the worker's age on the effective date of termination (see page 49) and from this date count back the worker's years of continuous service (see page 42). The maximum number of years they will take is 20.

(2) In working out the worker's weekly pay, the maximum the tribunal will take into account is £140.

(3) On that basis the award will be:

1½ weeks' pay for each year of service consisting wholly of weeks the worker was aged 41 or over.
1 week's pay for each year aged 22–40.
½ week's pay for each year below 22.

Men aged 64 and women aged 59 before the effective date of termination have the award reduced by one-twelfth for each complete month between reaching that age and the effective date of termination.

The maximum basic award will be £140 × 1½ × 20 = £4,200.

(4) The amount of any redundancy payment or other payment by the employer in respect of this award already received must be taken into account in calculating the basic award. In *Thomas v Betts Manufacturing Co. Ltd v Harding* (1978) IRLR 213 EAT, the EAT knocked down a basic ward of £82.40 as the tribunal had failed to take into account that Mrs Harding had received a redundancy payment (see also *Chelsea FC v Heath* (1981) IRLR 49 EAT).

(5) The tribunal can reduce a basic award:

- because the worker contributed to his or her dismissal;
- because the worker failed to minimise the loss caused by the dismissal;
- because the worker unreasonably refused an offer of re-instatement; or
- because of the worker's conduct before the dismissal which subsequently came to light.

Compensatory award

Where no order is made or it is not carried out, the worker is entitled to a compensatory award on top of the basic award. The purpose is to **compensate for the actual loss suffered as a result of the dismissal**. You will be able to argue for this award under the following heads, but subject to an overall limit on the compensatory award of £7,500.

Immediate loss of wages

Where the unfairly dismissed worker has been sacked without proper notice or without pay in lieu of notice she or he is entitled to be given **full net pay for the period of notice** to which she or he was entitled. Only income tax and national insurance contributions will be deducted from gross pay.

There is no deduction for wages received from another job during the period in which the worker was entitled to notice or to any social security benefit received:

■ Blackwell was entitled either to eight weeks' notice or to eight weeks' pay in lieu of notice because the tribunal found . . . the appellant had not been guilty of gross misconduct . . . the eight weeks represents an entitlement . . . the employee who is energetic enough and lucky enough to get a new job does not have to bring into account as the tribunal here thought that he did have to bring into account the wages paid by his new employers during that period (*Blackwell v GEC Elliott Process Automation Ltd* (1976) 11 ITR 103 EAT; see also *Blanchard v DRE Holdings (1971) Ltd* (1974) IRLR 266).

You will then want to claim compensation for loss of wages between the end of the period of due notice and the tribunal hearing for a worker who has not got a job or who has taken a lower-paid job. The basis of the calculation will be take-home pay, including overtime, multiplied by the number of weeks in the period. **Do not forget any post-dismissal wage rises.** From this will be deducted any extras received, such as an *ex gratia* severance payment. They will also take into account any failure to minimise loss.

Even a worker who is unfairly dismissed has a duty to make *reasonable* efforts to avoid unnecessary loss. She or he must act 'as a reasonable man would do if he had no hope of seeking compensation from his previous employer' (*Archbold's (Freightage) Ltd v Wilson* (1974) 9 ITR 133 NIRC).

A worker may have to accept a job, even if it is inferior to his or her own job and possibly even though she or he is seeking reinstatement.

A man who is dismissed from a £40 a week job may act unreasonably if he does not accept a job bringing in say £35 a week. If he does not do so a tribunal is fully entitled to say, 'we are going to take no account of any loss which one could have avoided by taking the £35 a week job' (*A. G. Bracey Ltd v Iles* (1973) IRLR 210).

On the other hand, if the claimant takes a job too lowly paid instead of shopping around for something better, he or she may be behaving unreasonably.

If the employer alleges failure to mitigate the loss, the onus of proof is on him or her to prove it. However, you should be armed with full details of letters of application, employers' replies and evidence as to the local employment situation to counter any allegations.

Recoupment

The tribunal should ignore any unemployment or supplementary benefit the worker has received in calculating loss of wages. This is not a windfall for the worker. You will probably hear the chairperson says something about recoupment regulations. The way the system works is as follows.

The tribunal is obliged to state the amount of the prescribed element in their award: that part of the compensatory award that relates to the period between the date of termination and the date of the award. The employer has to pay the rest of the compensation immediately but not this prescribed element.

The tribunal send the Department of Employment details of this element and they then serve on the employer a recoupment notice which claims back from him or her that part of the prescribed element that includes unemployment or supplementary benefit that the worker received between dismissal and hearing. The worker then receives the rest from the employer.

Future loss of wages

The tribunal here is involved in the difficult task of trying to predict the future. If its forecast is proved inaccurate it can only be overturned in exceptional circumstances (see page 233). You must ensure that the real life problems facing your member in finding a new job are brought to the tribunal's attention and that they do not take too optimistic a view of the chances of a fresh job.

If the worker has already got another lower-paid job, you will want the difference between the take-home pay in the old and new jobs. If the worker had been employed in his old job for a long time a tribunal may be willing to consider the difference over a longer period of four to five years (*Scottish Co-operative Wholesale Society Ltd v Lloyd* (1973) IRLR 93). The tribunal will take into account the time it may take to reach the level of the former job, whether it is likely that the worker may have lost income in the old job, say owing to illness (*Curtis v James Patterson (Darlington) Ltd* (1974) IRLR 88), and whether the new job represents the true earning capacity of the worker (*Donelly v Feniger and Blackburn Ltd* (1973) IRLR 26).

The picture is clearer where the worker has not got a job. **The onus of proof in showing future loss is on the worker.**

There must be some evidence of future loss and the scale of future loss to enable the tribunal to make an award . . . The tribunal must have something to bite on and if an applicant produces nothing he will only have himself to blame if he gets no compensation for loss of future earnings (*Adda International Ltd v Curcio* (1976) IRLR 425 EAT).

Details of the local position for workers of that kind are vital and you should suggest projections to the tribunal as to the length of time the worker will remain unemployed and the likely level of pay in a new job:

from our knowledge of the local employment position we consider that up to a year may elapse before the applicant can obtain employment with a level of earnings comparable with that which he enjoyed in his last employment. He may be successful in obtaining employment much earlier but at a much reduced level of earnings and we therefore think it proper to assess his loss over a period of a year (*Coleman v Tolemans Delivery Service Ltd* (1973) IRLR 67).

You should also point out any particular problems *this worker* will face. In one case, where a worker was sacked as a result of a fight which left him with a bad eye, the tribunal considered his loss as if he was in 'an uninjured state'. The EAT pointed out this was wrong, they should consider – 'how long the employee in his injured state was likely to remain unemployed, what kind of work he was likely to get when he was eventually re-employed and at what remuneration' (*Brittains Arborfield Ltd v Van Uden* (1977) ICR 211 EAT).

As workers cannot receive unemployment benefit for those weeks for which the tribunal have already compensated them for loss of future earnings, there is no question of deduction. You cannot generally claim compensation for the manner in which you were sacked. However, if this made a worker 'less acceptable to potential employers or exceptionally liable to selection for dismissal', it has been held that it should be considered (*Norton Tool Co. Ltd v Tewson* (1973) IRLR 86 NIRC). You can certainly argue that the manner of dismissal – for example, if there has been adverse publicity or if it was for trade-union reasons – should be taken as a factor in calculating future loss of earnings.

Loss of protection for unfair dismissal and redundancy and other statutory rights

The worker may find she or he will have to accumulate service before once more becoming protected by statutory rights. In practice, tribunals make no more than nominal awards for loss of statutory protection, usually £20.

Loss of other benefits

Under this heading tribunals have awarded compensation for loss of a company car (*Burnham v Yorkshire Engineering and Welding Company* (1973) IRLR 316); special travelling allowances (*De Cruz v Airways Aero Association Ltd* (1972) COIT 6066/72); coal allowances (*Dono v National Coal Board* (1972) COIT 12004/72); and loss of shares under a company scheme (*Bradshaw v Rugby Portland Cement* (1972) IRLR 46).

If you can think of any other benefits such as free meals or luncheon vouchers, you should have a go here. Bring evidence if there has been a loss of tips paid by customers or regular bonuses paid by your employer (see M. Cunningham, *Non-Wage Benefits*, Pluto Press).

Expenses

Legal expenses will *not* be allowed as part of a compensatory award. This would be costs under another guise (*Raynor v Remploy Ltd* (1973) IRLR 3). However, tribunals *have* allowed expenses incurred in looking around for another job (*Mathieson v Noble & Son Ltd* (1972) IRLR 76); the cost of moving from a tied cottage (*Butler v J. Wendon & Sons* (1972) IRLR 15); the cost of printing a curriculum vitae for applying for a new job (*Storey v American School in London Foundation Inc.* (1972) COIT 7452/72); and increased travelling expenses and removal expenses incurred in a new job (*Scottish Co-operative Wholesale Society Ltd v Lloyds* (1973) IRLR 93).

Loss of pension rights

'The burden of proving the loss and its extent lies fairly and squarely on the claimant notwithstanding that most of the evidence will be in the possession or power of the employer' (*Copson v Eversure Accessories Ltd* (1974) ICR 636 NIRC).

- If the employer will not collaborate, you should use the discovery procedure.
- Most unions now have specialists on pensions matters who should be able to help.

Absence of skilled advice imposes a duty upon industrial tribunals . . . If it is apparent that there is a pension scheme and that the details of that scheme are relevant the tribunal should tell the complainant that he is entitled to apply for an order requiring the employer to disclose these details. Tribunals should not hesitate in appropriate cases to determine the issue of liability as a preliminary point and then hear the evidence relevant to the assessment of compensation as an entirely separate issue (*Copson v Eversure Accessories Ltd*).

Do not gloss over the pension position because you think it is too involved. Quite a lot of money could be at stake. You should be particularly prepared if this is relevant as tribunals often leave the two sides to negotiate over this matter.

You can claim two kinds of pension loss:

(1) Loss of pension already earned

This will be made up of contributions paid by your employer and normally by you. Those over 26 who have contributed for five years since April 1975 will have a deferred pension with contributions frozen until retirement so there will be no loss.

If your employer has paid back your contributions (with interest) add up the employer's contributions. The contributions you have not received are called the 'capital sum'. Then take the rate of interest. To work out the rough amount divide the capital sum by the rate of interest. Add this amount to the capital sum to get a little above the total earned pension loss. If you are near retirement it is easier to take the total lump sum your pension would have been on retirement. Take away the contributions still due to give you the total loss of earned pension.

You may be able to transfer the pension to a new job, in which case there will be no loss.

(2) Loss of future pension

This is difficult to work out. Your new job, if and when you get one, may not have a pension scheme. So you lose the benefit of your new boss's contribution and you lose the benefit of not being able to pay your own contributions tax free. Your new pension scheme if it does exist may be different and not as good. Your loss will be the difference between the benefits you would have gained in the old scheme and the future benefits you will get in the new scheme, taking into account the relative amounts you and your boss pay in each situation.

You should look at: 'A Suggested Method For Assessing Pension Rights Under An Occupational Scheme Following A Finding Of Unfair Dismissal By An Industrial Tribunal'. This has been drawn up by the Government's Actuary Department and it is printed in the *Encyclopaedia of Labour Relation Law* (details at back of book; you can also get copies free from the Central Office of Tribunals and it will give you far more detail than we can include here).

Deductions for contributory fault

If the tribunal finds that a worker caused or contributed to his or her dismissal, then **they can reduce the compensatory award by a proportion which they consider just and equitable**.

The onus of proof here is on the employer. The tribunal can take a wide sweep and look at all the events leading up to the dismissal. However, there must be some fault or blameworthiness on the worker's part (*Morrish v Henlys (Folkestone) Garage Ltd* (1973) IRLR 61).

- Misconduct arising *after* the dismissal can now be taken into account under the 1980 Employment Act.
- There is *no maximum limit* to a finding of contributory

fault. The tribunal can find that a worker contributed 100 per cent to the dismissal so that he or she gets no compensation (*W. Devis & Sons Ltd v Atkins* (1977) IRLR 314 HL).

■ Maris, the superintendent of a cleansing department, was convicted of making fraudulent expenses claims. He was dismissed when other workers threatened industrial action. As the reason for dismissal was pressure from the workforce, the dismissal was unfair. However, as Maris was 'the author of his own misfortune', no compensation was awarded and the result was upheld on appeal (*Maris v Rotherham County Borough Council* (1974) IRLR 147 NIRC).

A week's pay

We have seen that in calculating a compensatory award the tribunal will take into account your net earnings in assessing a week's pay. The same is true of compensation for loss in time-off cases. With other rights, e.g. the basic award, the legislation provides a complicated method of calculating a week's pay.

Overtime

You can include overtime only where it is *contractual*, i.e. where the employer has a legal obligation to guarantee you the overtime and pay you, whether or not it is available, *and* where you have a legal obligation to work that overtime. In the majority of cases where clauses in collective agreements state 'such overtime shall be worked as the employer requires' you will have an obligation to work the overtime, but the employer will not have an obligation to provide it. It will not be contractual, and you cannot count overtime earnings in your week's pay. Bonuses will be included if they are contractual but tips, housing that goes with the job, and genuine expenses cannot be included, neither can payments for travelling time or payment in kind.

Hours

Time workers whose pay does not vary with the amount of work done will take as a week's pay the gross pay in the last week before notice, in dismissal cases, and the last week before absence begins, in relevant cases such as maternity.

Piece workers take as a week's pay the average of the last 12 weeks' gross pay from the date of dismissal or absence. Hours worked at overtime rate can be counted but at normal, not overtime, rate. You take 12 full weeks, not those, for example, in which you were laid off or sick.

Shift workers whose pay varies can calculate a week's pay in the same way and workers who have not worked 12 full weeks estimate a week's pay by the gross amounts they have received and the amounts similar workers have received.

Some workers, such as salespersons or lecturers, may have no fixed hours. Their week's pay is calculated by taking the average of the last 12 weeks they worked from the date proper notice was given, or if it was not, from the date of termination. In cases such as maternity and medical suspension the 12 weeks are calculated from the date immediately before absence. For more details see: J. McMullen, *Rights at Work*, Pluto Press.

Dismissal for union membership or activities

In these cases and where you have been unfairly selected for redundancy because of your union status, you will be entitled to a 'special award', a super-boosted revision of the additional award on top of the basic and compensatory awards.

You will not be entitled to a special award where:

- you have not asked for reinstatement/re-engagement;
- you have unreasonably refused an offer of suitable alternative employment as an alternative to redundancy;
- you have unreasonably ended a trial for a new job in a redundancy situation;
- you have started work under a renewed contract with your boss owing to an offer made before your redundancy within four weeks of your old contract ending.

You will be entitled to a special award of 104 weeks' pay subject to a maximum of £20,000 and a minimum of £10,000 where you asked for reinstatement or re-engagement but the tribunal did not order it. You will be entitled to a special award of 156 weeks' pay subject to a minimum of £15,000 but no maximum where your boss refuses to take you back when the tribunal so orders. Where reinstatement is ordered and the order is complied with, the tribunal can make an award based on loss sustained up to £7,500.

These awards are instead of additional awards. The £140 maximum for a week's pay does not apply but these awards *will* be reduced one twelfth for each complete month an employee is over 59/64. They *can* be reduced below the minimum if your conduct before or after dismissal merits it or if you unreasonably prevented reinstatement/re-engagement. A final point to remember about these cases: if you do not get your job back you have to receive a basic award subject to a minimum of £2,000.

The decision

The decision is normally given there and then. If the case is complicated or it is late in the day, the decision may be reserved. The decision, with reasons, is later put in writing. A copy is sent to:

- both parties;
- any others entitled to appear who did so, e.g. Secretary of State for Employment in a redundancy case;
- the EOC and the CRE in equal pay, sex discrimination or race relations cases.

A copy is also entered on the register at the regional office.

The decision must set out the findings of basic fact made by the tribunal. It *is not* obliged to make findings of fact on every peripheral fact in issue between the two sides (*Long and Hambly Ltd v Bryan* (1975) ICR 200 HC).

The tribunal can only decide on the basis of their findings of fact on the evidence before them (*A. W. Champion Ltd v Scobie* (1967) 2 ITR 411).

The decision must set out full and adequate reasons. In one case the decision simply read, 'The applicants were not redundant in accordance with any section of the Redundancy Payments Act. The evidence showed that dispute arose by reason of the alleged breach of the process trade agreement which is not within the jurisdiction of the tribunal.' On appeal, Lord Justice Parker said, 'I confess that I find that very unilluminating and it is certainly not the full reasons which a tribunal of this sort is supposed to give' (*Hanson v Wood Abington Process Engravers* (1968) 3 ITR 46 HC).

The reasons must deal with any question of law that was argued before the tribunal (*Seymour v Barber & Herron Ltd* (1970) 5 ITR 65 HC). Overall the decision must cover findings of fact on evidence with sufficient reasons to provide both parties with the details to enable them to know **whether or not they can appeal** (see Chapter 13).

A finding of fact or refusal to find a fact which no tribunal properly directed could reach on the basis of the evidence before it will give a right to appeal (*Alexander Machinery (Dudley) Ltd v Crabtree* (1974) 9 ITR 182 NIRC).

Where there is a majority decision in particular you may want to consider an appeal and the EAT has stated that the views of the majority and those of the minority should be set out clearly and distinctly in separate paragraphs (*Parkers Bakeries v Palmer* (1977) 12 ITR 111 EAT).

The EAT has suggested that to help those wishing to appeal and the tribunal, in all, **decisions should where possible cover:**

(1) The nature of the claim and the issues at contention.
(2) Numbered paragraphs of the facts found by the tribunal.
(3) The submissions made by both sides.
(4) A statement of the law the tribunal feels applies.
(5) The tribunal's conclusions (*Frank Charlesly & Co. v Sothern* (1979) EAT 437/79; *Allders International Ltd v Parkins* (1981) IRLR 68).

Tribunals must also set out details of compensation assessment, particularly reasons for reduction (*Pirelli General Cable Works Ltd v Murray* (1979) IRLR 190 EAT; *Savoia v Chiltern (Herts) Farms Ltd* (1981) IRLR 65 EAT).

Points to remember

(1) Make sure that you are familiar with your entitlements.
(2) Make sure you are clear as to whether or not your member wants the job back and there has been no last minute change.
(3) Have at hand detailed evidence of the employer's present and future labour force and changes in the job, e.g. wage rises since the dismissal.
(4) If the employer asks for an adjournment to think about reinstatement/re-engagement, and you gave adequate notice of this claim, ask for costs.
(5) Make sure the employer's arguments as to impracticability are justified. Argue that additional awards are intended to be punitive and therefore should be on the high side.
(6) Be prepared for any arguments on mitigation by producing documentary evidence on all job applications and replies, and details of the relevant labour market. Be prepared to take up any points on contribution.

(7) Make your own estimate on loss of future earnings. Do not wait for the tribunal or employer to do it for you. This is your last chance to help the member. Always look on the black side.

(8) Systematically tot up in detail any other benefits lost.

(9) Have full detailed documentation of any pension provision.

(10) If you disagree with the way the tribunal is assessing the compensation, or glossing over, or leaving out important matters, say so!

13.

Going further: enforcement, review and appeal

When you receive the written decision, read it very carefully. Is it as you understood at the hearing? Is the compensation correct? Does it meet the requirements laid down in Chapter 12? Have you got grounds for asking for a review or rehearing or appealing to a higher body? Are there likely to be problems in getting the employer to accept the decision? In this chapter we look at the rules on how you can enforce tribunal awards and how you can take your case further if you are dissatisfied with the decision.

Where to find the law
County Court Rules 1936 Order 25, Rule 7A
Industrial Tribunals Regulations 9, 10
EP(C)A ss. 135, 136
Employment Appeal Tribunal Rules

Enforcing the decision

Most tribunal orders are carried out. There is not a great enforcement problem. **The tribunals have no enforcement machinery.** In unfair dismissal cases if the employer refused to pay the compensation awarded by the tribunal, you would have to go to the County Court. Wait about a fortnight for the employer to pay up. If there is no reply or appeal from the employer within 42 days, write again threatening legal action unless the award is paid in seven days. **If this does not work:**

- apply to the County Court in the district in which the employer carries on business. You do not need to let the employer know, and he or she does not need to be involved;

- let the County Court have a copy of the decision, together with a sworn statement verifying the amount of compensation;
- the registrar of the County Court can then make an order on your application. The registrar has a discretion to allow the employer a certain period in which to pay and might do this if the employer is appealing. The order can also include any fees or costs;
- if the employer does not cough up at this stage, the order becomes an order of the County Court;
- it can then be enforced by seizing and selling the employer's goods or by ensuring that the money is paid in specified instalments.

In Scotland you apply to the Sheriff Court in the employer's district to have the award automatically enforced. A copy of the decision certified by the tribunal will be enough, there is no need as in England and Wales for a separate court order. There is also a procedure by which a decree of the Sheriff Court can be registered in and enforced by a County Court and vice versa (Inferior Courts Judgement Extension Act 1882).

If the employer is bankrupt or goes into liquidation you should apply to the receiver or liquidator for payment. If there are problems in respect of cases involving redundancy guarantees, payments award, medical suspension, time off and basic awards in unfair dismissal cases, the Secretary of State has the power to pay you in full out of the redundancy fund.

Altering the decision

The regulations give the chairperson the right to correct any clerical mistakes or errors in the written decision which have been caused by accidental slips. Corrections must be accompanied by a signed certificate. However, if it is not this obvious unarguable kind of slip, can the tribunal change its decision if it finds it has made a mistake?

■ At the end of a tribunal hearing the chairman announced that a woman was entitled to a redundancy payment and awarded £532. Several days later before the document containing the decision had been drawn up, the chairperson realised that a case cited had not been properly considered. He asked the parties to come back to put forward further arguments. The woman appealed on the grounds that a final decision had been made. The EAT held that the practice in other courts should be followed – before a decision had been drawn up it could be altered (*Hanks v Ace High Productions Ltd* (1979) IRLR 32 EAT).

The rule now as laid down in *Hanks* is that a decision can be altered at any time before it is registered and sent to the parties, but if a new point is raised the parties should be given a chance to be heard.

Reviews and appeals

We now go on to explain the different situations in which you should ask for a review or an appeal. The EAT has taken a flexible attitude and outlined situations in which on grounds of speed and convenience a review may be substituted for an appeal:

From time to time we have appeals sometimes in relation to small matters of compensation, sometimes in relation to matters where there has been a slip or error of law . . . and the mistakes come to light quite soon after the hearing. It seems to us that the correct course is for such mistakes when they occur and are recognised to be corrected by review rather than appeal because the appeal takes much longer and is much more expensive (*British Midland Airways Ltd v Lewis* (1978) ICR 782 EAT).

A tribunal can hear an application for a review even though an application for an appeal has been made. The chairperson should get in touch with the registrar of the EAT, however, to discuss the position. As the hearing of the review will normally be before the appeal, a review, the EAT has said, may be useful in removing or limiting the grounds for appeal or the findings of fact (*Dean v Polytechnic of North London* (1973) 8 ITR 526 NIRC: *Blackpole Ltd v Sullivan* (1978) ICR 558 EAT).

Applying for a review

● There is no standard form but you should apply in writing stating fully not only the grounds on which a review is sought, but also a statement of the grounds on which you believe that the original statement is wrong (*Drakard v Wilton* (1977) 12 ITR 170 EAT).

● You must apply for a review either at the hearing or any

time afterwards provided the application is made within **14 days of the date the decision is sent** to the parties.

- The time limit can be extended but you should have a good reason given that the other side is entitled to treat the decision as final. The decision will be taken by the chairperson or the tribunal.

Grounds for a review

(1) The decision was wrongly made as the result of an error on the part of the tribunal staff

There are no reported cases of reviews under this heading. There might be grounds for a review, for example, where the tribunal staff failed to inform witnesses of the hearing, or where you were given insufficient notice of the hearing.

(2) A party did not receive notice of the proceedings leading to the decision

This would cover the situation where you were not informed of the hearing, or where either side did not receive copies of any of the relevant documents, such as the IT1 or IT3, or copies of the decision.

(3) The decision was made in the absence of a party or person entitled to be heard

If one side fails to turn up the tribunal can hear the case, dismiss it or adjourn it to a later date. If they hear it in your absence and find against your side, or dismiss the application, you may have grounds for review, arguing that they exercised their discretion wrongly.

You will have to show good reasons why you could not appear or ask for a postponement, and a major concern of the chairperson in deciding whether a review should be granted under this heading is whether the proceedings have been significantly impaired by the fact that one side has not been present.

- A worker wrote to the tribunal stating he was unable to attend through sickness. He did not know he could apply for an adjournment. The assistant secretary wrote back recommending that he should appear but failing to mention that he could apply for an adjournment. In his absence the tribunal found the dismissal fair. His application for a review was refused on the grounds that he could have asked for a postponement, there was no new evidence and he was simply trying to re-argue his case. He appealed against the refusal to grant a review on the grounds that the tribunal had drawn inferences against him regarding his ability to work which they would not have done had he been present. The EAT stated that he should have been told that he could ask for postponement and he had some basis for arguing that if he had been there the tribunal would not have found that his ability to work was impaired by ill health. The case should be sent back to the tribunal with instructions to consider the application for a review (*Holland v Cyprane* (1977) ICR 355 EAT).

(4) New evidence has become available since the decision — provided that its existence could not have been reasonably known of or foreseen

The kind of guidelines the tribunals will follow are those Lord Denning listed:

> first it must be shown that the evidence could not have been obtained with reasonable diligence for use at the trial; second the evidence must be such that if given it would probably have an important influence on the result of the case although it need not be decisive; third the evidence must be such as is presumably to be believed or in other words it must be apparently credible although it need not be incontrovertible (*Ladd v Marshall* (1954) 3 AER 745 CA).

If you apply for a review under this heading then *you must* let the tribunal have a detailed written statement of the evidence that you wish to introduce (*Vauxhall Motors Ltd v Henry* (1978) 13 ITR 332 EAT).

Problems have occurred where, after compensation has been assessed by the tribunal on certain principles, the basis on which they decided changes. For example, a worker told the tribunal that he had a new job and compensation was calculated on that basis. A few weeks later he was out of work. In this kind of case, where events *quickly* undermine the tribunal's forecast, the tribunal can review the situation and change its decision to take account of the new evidence (*Bateman v British Leyland (UK) Ltd* (1974) IRLR 101 NIRC).

But note – if the worker has been *paid* the amount due as the tribunal award, there can be no review because the employer has discharged the debt and the cause of action cannot be renewed.

(5) The interests of justice require such a review

The idea of this category is not to provide a 'hold all' for cases which you can't squeeze into any of the other headings. For example, if the evidence you wish to bring up at a review was within your knowledge at the time of the original hearing, and you can't therefore get within the 'new evidence category', you cannot just generally assert that the broad interests of justice demand a rehearing. The interests of justice are:

(1) your interest in wanting a rehearing;
(2) your opponent's interest in having got a result and feeling that should be final;
(3) the interest of the public that the tribunal decision should be as final as possible.

■ Flint, a redundant worker, was offered alternative employment which involved leaving 25 minutes earlier and walking a mile to and from transport. His refusal to accept it was held to be unreasonable. He applied for a review on the ground that he suffered from a bad leg which made the walk more difficult. He mentioned this to the union official for the first time after the decision. The chairperson held that there should be no review and this was upheld on appeal. It would have failed under 'new evidence' and it needed 'some special additional factor' for a case like this to require a review (*Flint v Eastern Electricity Board* (1975) 10 ITR 152 HC).

A review might be granted under this heading to correct simple errors, or where you consider that there was not a fair hearing (see page 236), or even where there was an error of law (*Namyslo v Secretary of State for Employment* (1979) IRLR 450).

The hearing

(1) The application is considered by the chairperson of the tribunal who decided the case, or by a regional chairperson. The chairperson can refuse the application if she or he thinks it has no reasonable prospect of success. If your application for a review gives inadequate reasons, the chairperson should give you a chance to elaborate, before rejecting your application (*Drakard & Sons Ltd v Wilton* (1977) ICR 642 EAT). If he or she turns you down, you can appeal to EAT on a point of law against his decision. You will receive a written decision refusing the review with brief reasons.

If you are asking for a decision of a chairperson to be reviewed, for example, if he or she has refused you discovery of documents, then the application at this stage will be heard by a full tribunal.

(2) If the chairperson does not refuse the application, it will then be heard by a full tribunal. This will be the same tribunal that heard your case, unless it is impossible to get the same three people together, in which case a different tribunal will hear your application. The chairperson cannot *grant* a review, although he or she can *refuse* one. You will be given the date of a short hearing which will hear arguments by both sides. The tribunal may refuse a review, vary the decision or revoke the decision and order a re-hearing.

Normally, the tribunal will make arrangements for a future hearing, although if it varies the decision it can do so there and then. This is not common and the letter from the tribunal giving you details of the appointment should state whether the hearing will simply decide whether there should be a re-hearing at some future date, or proceed there and then to look at the issues you want reviewed if the application is successful. If this happens and you are unprepared for a hearing, you can ask for an adjournment.

(3) If an order is made for a review it will specify:

- whether the re-hearing is to be by the same or by another tribunal. If the tribunal which ordered the re-hearing revoked the original decision it is better to have a fresh tribunal hearing the case. If it is a re-hearing ordered by the EAT to find certain extra facts or to re-calculate the compensation, the re-hearing will normally take place before the original tribunal; and
- whether only a certain part of the decision should be reviewed, or a certain area of evidence re-examined. If the order is not specific on this point then the extent of the review will be in the discretion of the tribunal at the re-hearing.

A tribunal *can* review the whole decision, not only that part specifically mentioned in the application; or it can limit the review to a particular point.

The procedure at a re-hearing will be the same as at an original hearing. A tribunal cannot hear a second application for a review based on the same grounds as an earlier application. **A refusal is final** (*Stevenson (Dyers) Ltd v Brennan* (1974) ICR 194 NIRC).

Complaints of bias

Workers sometimes appeal against decisions on the ground that they feel that the tribunal was biased against them.

■ Gerry Healy claimed unfair dismissal. On the second day of the hearing he requested a fresh hearing before a different tribunal. The tribunal had cut short his cross-examination of certain witnesses and he stated that 'he had no confidence in the fairness of the tribunal'. The tribunal pointed out that all that had been stopped in cross-examination was the constant repetition of the same questions but they agreed to a fresh hearing. The employers appealed and the EAT agreed that the tribunal was wrong. A person's lack of confidence in a tribunal was too wide a ground to allow the tribunal to exercise its power to order a fresh hearing. Using this device a person could constantly demand a fresh tribunal when things appeared to be going badly for his or her case (*Automobile Proprietary Ltd v Healy* (1979) ICR 809 EAT).

The EAT will be reluctant to uphold allegations that tribunals have acted in a biased way, and a general complaint of bias is not going to get you very far. You need to tie the tribunal's behaviour down to some specific breach of the regulations or practice.

- If you are appealing on grounds of prejudice or bias, you need to set out full particulars.
- If you do complain, the EAT registrar will contact you to ask whether you wish to proceed with the complaint. He or she may ask you for written affidavits on the complaint and further particulars.
- The EAT registrar will provide all documentation for the tribunal chairperson to comment on and all particulars will be provided for the other side.

Review by High Court

The industrial tribunals are also subject to the supervisory powers of the courts exercised through a series of legal orders in exceptional cases.

■ Three workers claimed unfair dismissal and redundancy. One tribunal member held that they were unfairly dismissed not redundant. The second decided they were redundant not unfairly dismissed. The third thought that they were neither redundant nor unfairly dismissed! The chairperson in a written decision stated that the tribunal's decision was that the case should be reheard by another tribunal. The employer argued that a majority had found that the workers were neither unfairly dismissed or redundant. They therefore went to the High Court for an order to stop the fresh tribunal hearing the case.

The court held that tribunals had an inherent power to refer their decision to a different tribunal if the disagreement of the members or other factors meant that the result of the hearing would be inconclusive or ineffectual, and that was the position here (*R v Industrial Tribunal ex parte Cotswold Collotype Co. Ltd* (1979) ICR 190 HC).

Grounds for appeal

You can only appeal where you feel that the tribunal decision shows an error of law (see page 14).

To win an appeal you are going to have to show that the tribunal:

(1) misdirected itself in law, or misunderstood the law, or misapplied the law. For example, it may have wrongly interpreted a section of an act or wrongly exercised its discretion to grant a postponement;
(2) came to a decision without taking into account relevant evidence, or misunderstood that evidence, or without evidence to support what they found as fact; or
(3) came to a decision that no reasonable tribunal could have reached.

The EAT will be extremely reluctant to interfere with a decision. They will *not do so* where they themselves would have come to a different decision, if they feel that there was evidence on which a tribunal *could* have arrived at the decision (*Retarded Children's Society Ltd v Day* (1978) ICR 437 CA).

- If you feel that the tribunal followed the incorrect procedure or the hearing was improperly conducted, that will be enough to raise a point of law (see page 14).
- If the tribunal have incorrectly calculated compensation or not given details of how the figure was arrived at, that too is

FORM I

EMPLOYMENT PROTECTION ACT 1975

NOTICE OF APPEAL FROM DECISION OF INDUSTRIAL TRIBUNAL

1.   The appellant is /name and address of appellant/:-

2.   Any communication relating to this appeal may be sent to the appellant at /appellant's address for service, including telephone number, if any/:-

3.   The appellant appeals from
/here give particulars of the decision of the industrial tribunal from which the appeal is brought/:-

on the following questions of law:-
/here set out the question of law on which the appeal is brought/.

4.   The parties to the proceedings before the industrial tribunal, other than the appellant, were /names and addresses of other parties - and of their representatives if applicable - to the proceedings resulting in decision appealed from/:-

5.   The appellant's grounds of appeal are:-
/here state the grounds of appeal/.

6.   A copy of the industrial tribunal's decision is attached to this notice.

Date: ....   Signed: ....

Form EAT1

a point of law (see Chapter 12). However, the EAT have recently pointed out that the 'Appeal Tribunal will not interfere with awards of compensation unless the error is shown to be something which could be described as more than trifling' (*Fougere v Phoenix Motor Co. (Surrey) Ltd* (1976) ICR 495 EAT; see also *Blackwell v GEC Elliott Process Automation Ltd* (1976) ITR 103 EAT). In these kinds of cases you should first seek a review. Remember Legal Aid is available for individuals who appeal.

Time limits

You should have carefully considered the matter and examined the law before deciding on an appeal. As soon as the case is concluded, you should make a tentative decision on appeal which you can change or reinforce on receiving the written decision. You must be in a position to give detailed grounds for your appeal. Failure to do so can lead to rejection or delay through the EAT requesting further details.

Even if you are going to argue the case before the EAT, **get your union's legal advisers to look at the decision as soon as it arrives**. They will be useful in formulating your notice of appearance on the lines the EAT requires.

You must appeal to the EAT **within 42 days of the date on which the tribunal decision was sent to you**. You will see this date at the end of the decision and it is included in the computation.

Unlike tribunals, the EAT have a complete discretion to extend the time limit (*Wilson v Fine Arts* (1982) EAT 471/82), but they are fairly strict. The reason for this is that you have had one bite of the cherry, and there is less reason for giving you a second chance than if you had never had a trial at all. Extensions will only be granted in 'rare and exceptional cases' (*Marshall v Harland & Wolff Ltd* (1972) 7 ITR 132 NIRC).

If the tribunal gives a decision but leaves the question of compensation until later, you must apply for an appeal **within 42 days of the decision** and not wait for assessment of compensation (*Hem v Sykes & Sons Ltd,* EAT; *The Times*, 25 October 1978). If you do get an extension, therefore, it is likely to be with costs against you (*Young v Scot Meat Products Ltd* (1978) EAT 783/78).

Before the hearing

As with the tribunal, **there is a vetting procedure:**

- if your appeal is rejected, you have the right to send in a **fresh notice of appeal** with the unexpired part of the 42 day time limit, or within 28 days of the rejection by the registrar, whichever is the longest.
- **A preliminary hearing** can be held. Your opponent will be informed of this but is not required to attend and is not permitted to take part. Your job at the hearing is to satisfy the tribunal that you have an arguable point of law.

You can insist that your case go forward but this might mean costs awarded against you.

If your case *does* proceed **the registrar will inform your opponent**. A date will be set by which the other side must reply stating reasons for opposing the appeal. The employer may simply cite the tribunal decision as reasons. If there is no reply within the specified time, the other side may be barred from taking any further part in the proceedings.

In some cases **where one side appeals against the decision, the other side may cross-appeal**, i.e. appeal against part of the decision which they feel unfavourable to them. Where there is a finding of unfair dismissal, an employer may appeal against the decision; the worker may appeal against the compensation findings. If your opponent cross-appeals, the tribunal will write to you setting a date by which you must reply.

The chairperson of the industrial tribunal is under a duty to take a **note of the substance of the evidence** (*Archbold's (Freightage) Ltd v Wilson* (1974) 9 ITR 133 NIRC). This is useful in removing any doubts in the decision and in supplementing it, and it is supplied by the regional office to the EAT when they have been informed that an appeal is pending. **You cannot get hold of this note** in order to decide whether or not to appeal. 'Those notes are supplied for the use of the appeal tribunal and are not for the parties to embark on a fishing expedition to establish further grounds for appeal' (*Practice Direction* March (1978) 1 AER 293 EAT).

You will only be able to get hold of the chairperson's notes if you can show why they are necessary for the purpose of your appeal. You will have to specify exactly what finding of fact in the decision you are attacking, or which findings of fact you feel ought to have been made on the evidence (*EAT Practice Direction* 17/2/81; *Webb v Anglian Water Authority* (1981) IRLR 494 EAT).

Applications on matters such as witness orders or documents are dealt with by the registrar. The registrar or the judge involved with the case may call the parties to a meeting to give directions, i.e. to decide how the case will be handled, the way in which evidence should be given, or the amendment of any documents.

If you wish to appeal against the decision of the registrar on these matters the objection will be heard by a judge who may decide on it or refer it to a full EAT. If you wish to appeal you must give verbal or written notice **within three days of the date of the registrar's decision** and he or she must let you know the arrangements for the appeal.

Any party failing to comply with the orders of the EAT can be debarred from taking any further part in the proceedings. If there is an application to bar one side it will usually be heard on the day of the full hearing immediately before it.

The hearing

Normally, the case will be listed once your opponent's answer has been received and sent to you. A list of cases to be heard on specified dates during the next calendar month is drawn up at the start of each month and other cases are warned to be on standby. **You will, therefore, have between four and eight weeks' notice.**

It is your job to make sure that all exhibits and documents used before the tribunal are sent to the EAT.

If you wish to introduce new documents you should apply to the registrar. Normally the EAT does *not* allow the introduction of fresh evidence, which might have been given at the original hearing, into an appeal which is dealing solely with **questions of law**. However, it has been held that **fresh evidence will be allowed:**

(1) if a reasonable explanation can be given for the fact that it was not produced at the original hearing;
(2) it is credible; and
(3) it would or could have had a decisive effect on the tribunal's decision (*Bagga v Heavy Electricals (India) Ltd* (1972) ICR 118 NIRC).

The hearing will normally be in public with the parties present. However, if the legal issues at stake have been clearly sifted out in the pre-hearing procedure, the case may simply be heard through written submissions. The grounds for asking for a private hearing are the same as those applying to industrial tribunals (see page 163).

Like the tribunals, the EAT is given full scope to regulate its own procedure. The rules specifically state that failure to follow them will *not* invalidate the hearing and that the EAT can *vary* the procedure. The procedure will follow that outlined for tribunals (see page 171). **Normally the EAT will:**

- **dismiss** the appeal or **allow** it. The EAT have the power to reverse the tribunal decision in full or in part.
- **send the case back** for a re-hearing in whole or part by the industrial tribunal which heard it, giving advice in laying down legal principles to govern the hearing.

The EAT will remit a case where they feel 'not necessarily that something has gone wrong but that at least it looks very likely that something may have gone wrong'. Where there is a need for further investigation the EAT take the line that 'the best people to do that are the tribunals' (*Askew v Victoria Sporting Club* (1976) ICR 302 EAT).

You can appeal further to the Court of Appeal with the leave of the EAT or CA. This will not suspend the enforcement of the EAT decision unless you apply to the EAT and they specifically direct suspension pending appeal.

You can *within 14 days* of an EAT order being made apply for a review on the grounds that:

(1) the order was wrongly made as a result of an error on the part of the tribunal or its staff;
(2) a party did not receive proper notice of the proceedings; or
(3) the interests of justice require a review.

The EAT can award costs where proceedings are 'unnecessary, improper or vexatious or there has been unreasonable delay or other unreasonable conduct in bringing or conducting the proceedings'.

As with tribunals, costs are on the increase in the more legal atmosphere of the EAT. The EAT have said that an appeal is 'unnecessary' if its outcome can make no difference to the situation of the parties (*C. W. Coates & Sons Ltd v Kendrick* (1979) EAT 178/79). The test seems to be, has your case **a reasonable prospect of success?** In *Spiller French Holdings Ltd v Green and Miotk* (1979) EAT 704/79, the EAT argued that although the appellants' lawyers had advised that they had an arguable case 'this was not equivalent to a reasonable prospect of success' and costs were awarded.

Costs will be awarded if you simply appeal on issues of fact and persist in taking the case to a hearing (*Gilmour v J. & A. Gardner & Co. Ltd* (1979) EAT 23/79). If you allege bias on the part of the tribunal but make no attempt to substantiate this (*Adamson v Howard Doris Ltd* (1978) EAT 434/78), or if you delay and then withdraw the appeal only eight or nine days before the date fixed for a hearing (*TVR Engineering Ltd v Johnson* (1978) EAT 198/78).

Points to remember

(1) If relevant, raise the question of a review *straight away*, otherwise check carefully the written decision immediately you receive it.

(2) If you feel that you have any grounds for review or appeal, send the decision and relevant papers as quickly as possible to the union legal department or advisers.

(3) Remember the short time limits; you have to decide *very quickly* on a review or appeal.

(4) Seriously consider an appeal if it is a split decision with the chairperson on your side. Appeal generally if it is a split decision.

(5) Discuss the position with the member and make sure that the union supports going further.

(6) In areas where there is an overlap between review and appeal, assess which is most suitable for you, remember to follow the correct procedure for each.

(7) Remember legal aid *is available* for appeals.

Useful addresses

Where to get solicitors' names

England and Wales
New Legal Aid
P. O. Box 9
Nottingham NG1 6DS

Scotland
Legal Aid Central Committee
P. O. Box 123
21 Drumsheugh Gardens
Edinburgh EH3 7YR

Organisations

Advisory, Conciliation and Arbitration Service

Head office
11–12 St James Square
London SW1Y 4LA
tel: 01-214 6000

Northern Region
Westgate House
Westgate Road
Newcastle upon Tyne NE1 1TJ
tel: 0632 612191

Yorkshire and Humberside Region
Commerce House
St Albans Place
Leeds LS2 8HH
tel: 0532 431371

South East Region
Clifton House
83–117 Euston Road
London NW1 2RB
tel: 01-388 5100

South West Region
16 Park Place
Clifton
Bristol BS8 1JP
tel: 0272 211921

Midlands Region
Alpha Tower
Suffolk Street
Queensway
Birmingham B1 1TZ
tel: 021-643 9911

North Western Region
Boulton House
17–21 Chorlton Street
Manchester M1 3NY
tel: 061-228 3222

Scotland
123–57 Bothwell Street
Glasgow G2 7DY
tel: 041-204 2677

Wales
Phase 1
Ty Glas Road
Llanishen
Cardiff CF4 5PH
tel: 0222 762636

N. Ireland
Labour Relations Agency
Windsor House
9–15 Bedford Street
Belfast BT2 7MU
tel: Belfast 21442

Central Arbitration Committee
1 The Abbey Garden
Great College Street
London SW1
tel: 01-222 8571

Central Office of the Industrial Tribunals

England and Wales
93 Ebury Bridge Road
London SW1
tel: 01-730 9161

Scotland
St Andrew House
141 West Nile Street
Glasgow G1 2RU
tel: 041-331 1601

N. Ireland
2nd Floor
Bedford House
Bedford Street
Belfast BT2 7NR
tel: Belfast 27666

Regional Offices of Industrial Tribunals

Aberdeen
252 Union Street
Aberdeen AB1 1TN
tel: 0224 52307

Ashford
Tufton House
Tufton Street
Ashford
Kent TN23 1RJ
tel: 0233 21346

Birmingham
Phoenix House
1–3 Newall Street
Birmingham B3 3NH
tel: 021-236 6051

Bristol
43–51 Price Street
Bristol BS1 4PE
tel: 0272 298261

Bury St Edmunds
118 Northgate Street
Bury St Edmunds
Suffolk IP33 1HQ
tel: 0284 62171

Cardiff
Caradog House
1–3 St Andrew's Place
Cardiff CF1 3BE
tel: 0222 372693

Dundee
13 Albert Square
Dundee DD1 1DD
tel: 0382 21578

Edinburgh
11 Melville Crescent
Edinburgh EH3 7LU
tel: 031-226 5584

Exeter
Renslade House
Bonhay Road
Exeter EX4 3BX
tel: 0392 79665

Leeds
Minerva House
East Parade
Leeds LS1 5JZ
tel: 0532 459741

Liverpool
1 Union Court
Cook Street
Liverpool L2 4UJ
tel: 051-236 9397

London (North)
19–29 Woburn Place
London WC1
tel: 01-632 4921

London (South)
93 Ebury Bridge Road
London SW1W 8RE
tel: 01-730 9161

Manchester
Alexandra House
14–22 The Parsonage
Manchester M3 2JA
tel: 061-833 0581

Newcastle
Watson House
Pilgrim Street
Newcastle on Tyne NE1 6RB
tel: 0632 28865

Nottingham
Birkbeck House
Trinity Square
Nottingham
tel: 0602 45701

Sheffield
Fargate Court
Fargate
Sheffield S1 2HU
tel: 0742 70348

Southampton
Dukes Keep
Marsh Lane
Southampton SO1 1EX
tel: 0703 39555

Employment Appeal Tribunal

England and Wales
4 St James Square
London SW1
tel: 01-214 6000
01-214 3367

Scotland
249 West George Street
Glasgow G2 4QE
tel: 041-248 6213

Companies House

England and Wales
55 City Road
London EC1
tel: 01-253 9393

Scotland
102 George Street
Edinburgh EH2 3DG
tel: 031-225 5774

N. Ireland
43–47 Chichester Street
Belfast BT1 4RJ
tel: 0232 34121

Commission for Racial Equality
Elliott House
10–12 Allington Street
London SW1
tel: 01-828 7022

HMSO Bookshops

London
49 High Holborn
London WC1V 6HB

Birmingham
258 Broad Street
Birmingham B1 2HE

Bristol
Southey House
Wine Street
Bristol BS1 2BQ

Manchester
Brazenose Street
Manchester M60 8AS

Edinburgh
13A Castle Street
Edinburgh EH2 3AR

Cardiff
41 The Hayes
Cardiff CF1 1JW

Belfast
80 Chichester Street
Belfast BT1 4SY

Incomes Data Services
140 Great Portland Street
London W1N 5TA
tel: 01-580 0521

Incorporated Council of Law Reporting for England and Wales
3 Stone Buildings
Lincolns Inn
London WC2A 3XN
tel: 01-246 6471

Industrial Relations Services
67 Maygrove Road
London NW6 2ES
tel: 01-238 4751–6

Labour Research Department
78 Blackfriars Road
London SE1
tel: 01-928 3649

Equal Opportunities Commission
Overseas House
Quay Street
Manchester M3 3HM
tel: 061-833 9244

Health and Safety Commission
Bayards House
2 Chepstow Place
London W2
tel: 01-229 3456

Department of Employment Regional Offices

Head Office
8 St James's Square
London SW1Y 4JR
tel: 01-214 6000

Midlands Region
2 Duchess Place
Hadley Road
Fiveways
Birmingham B16 8NS
tel: 021-455 7111

Northern Region
93a Grey Street
Newcastle on Tyne NE1 6HE
tel: 0632 27575

North Western Region
Sunley Buildings
Picadilly Plaza
Manchester M60 7JS
tel: 061-832 9111

**South Eastern Region and
London Region**
Clifton House
83–117 Euston Road
London NW1 2RB
tel: 01-388 5100

South Western Region
The Pithay
Bristol BS1 2NQ
tel: 0272 291071

**Yorkshire and Humberside
Region**
City House
Leeds LS1 4JH
tel: 0532 38232

Scotland
43 Jeffrey Street
Edinburgh EH1 1UU
tel: 031-556 8433

Wales
Companies House
Crown May
Maindy
Cardiff CF4 3UW
tel: 0222 388588

Legal Aid

England and Wales
P. O. Box 9
Nottingham NG1 6DS
tel: 0602 42341 (area office)
        0602 40327 (local office)

Scotland
Legal Aid Central Committee
P. O. Box 123
Edinburgh EH3 7YR
tel: 031-226 7411

**National Council for Civil
Liberties**
186 Kings Cross Road
London WC1X 9DE
tel: 01-278 3259

**National Association of
Citizens Advice Bureaux**
110 Drury Lane
London WC2
tel: 01-836 9231

Trade Union Congress
Congress House
Great Russell Street
London WC1B 3CS
tel: 01-636 4030

Wages Councils
12 St James Square
London SW1Y 4LL
tel: 01-405 8454

Further reading

On the background to law

ACAS, *Conciliation in Complaints by Individuals to Industrial Tribunals*, 1982.

J. Griffiths, *The Politics of the Judiciary*, Fontana, 1980.

A. Paterson, *The Law Lords*, Macmillan, 1982.

R. Miliband, *State in Capitalist Society*, Quartet Books, 1980.

B. Weekes *et al.*, *Industrial Relations And The Limits Of Law*, Blackwell, 1975.

Detailed books about labour law

Employment Law Handbook, Butterworth, 1979.

C. Grunfeld, *The Law of Redundancy*, Sweet & Maxwell, 1980.

B. A. Hepple, *Hepple and O'Higgins Employment Law*, Sweet & Maxwell, 1981.

Labour Relations Statutes and Materials, Sweet & Maxwell, 1979.

Law at Work, Fourteen Concise Guides, Sweet & Maxwell, 1981.

J. McMullen, *Rights At Work*, Pluto Press, 2nd edn, 1983.

National Association of Citizens Advice Bureaux, *Social Security Appeals*, 1980.

R. W. Rideout, *Principles of Labour Law*, Sweet & Maxwell, 1981.

The CRE, EOC and DE also publish a detailed series of pamphlets on your legal rights which may be helpful.

For keeping up with labour law

Croners Employment Law, six-monthly updates (Croner Publishing).

B. A. Hepple and P. O'Higgins, *Encyclopaedia of Labour Relations Law*, three loose-leaf volumes regularly updated (Sweet & Maxwell).

For keeping up with cases

Incomes Data Services produce fortnightly *Briefs* and regular *Supplements* and *Handbooks* covering short digest on tribunal cases.

Industrial Relations Services produce a fortnightly *Industrial Relations Legal Information Bulletin* which covers similar ground.

A very useful collection of cases is J. McGlyne, *Unfair Dismissal Cases*, Butterworth, 1980.

The Industrial Law Journal, published quarterly by Sweet & Maxwell has longer articles on labour law.

For full case transcripts, etc.

Industrial Cases Reports or *Industrial Relations Law Reports*.

More about industrial tribunals

J. Angel, *How To Prepare Yourself For An Industrial Tribunal*, Institute of Personnel Management, 1981.

M. J. Goodman, *Industrial Relations Procedure*, Oyez, 1979.

J. Mulhern and I. McLean, *The Industrial Tribunal, A Practical Guide To Employment Law And Tribunal Procedure*, Barry Rose, 1982.

D. B. Williams and D. J. Walker, *Industrial Tribunals Practice And Procedure*, Butterworth, 1980.

For a detailed look at practice and procedure in Scotland and the Six Counties

W. Leslie, *Industrial Tribunal Practice in Scotland*, Green & Son, 1981.

Phyllis Bateson and John McKee, *Industrial Tribunals in Northern Ireland*, Law in Action Series, Queens University Press, 1981.

List of Statutes, Regulations and Codes

Statues
Inferior Courts Judgement Extension Act 1882
Factories Act 1961
Contracts of Employment Act 1963
Industrial Training Act 1964
Redundancy Payments Act 1965
Equal Pay Act 1970
Industrial Relations Act 1971
Contracts of Employment Act 1972
Health and Safety at Work Act 1974
Trade Union and Labour Relations Act 1974
Social Security Act 1975
Litigants in Person (Costs and Expenses) Act 1975
Social Security Pensions Act 1975
Sex Discrimination Act 1975
Employment Protection Act 1975
Trade Union and Labour Relations (Amendment) Act 1976
Supplementary Benefits Act 1976
Race Relations Act 1976
Employment Protection (Consolidation) Act 1978
Employment Act 1980
Employment Act 1982

Regulations
Occupational Pension Schemes Regulations 1975
Occupational Pension Schemes Regulations 1976
Sex Discrimination (Questions and Replies) Order 1975 (SI 1975 No 2048)
Employment Protection (Recoupment of Unemployment Benefit and
    Supplementary Benefit Regulations) 1977 (SI 1977 No 674)
Race Relations (Questions and Replies) Order 1977 (SI 1977 No 842)
Litigants in Person (Costs and Expenses) Order 1980 (SI 1980 No 1159)
Industrial Tribunals (Rules of Procedure) Regulations 1980 (SI 1980 No 884)
Industrial Tribunals (Rules of Procedure) Scotland Regulations 1980 (SI
    1980 No 885)
Industrial Tribunals (Rules of Procedure) N. Ireland 1981 (SI 1981 No 188)
Employment Appeal Tribunal Rules 1980 (SI 1980 No 2035)
Practice Direction (EAT Appeals) 1981 1 AER 583
Transfer of Undertakings (Protection of Employment) Regulations 1981

Codes
Code of Practice on Industrial Relations (produced by DE under Industrial
    Relations Act but still operative)
Disciplinary Practice and Procedures in Employment ACAS Code No 1
Disclosure of Information to Trade Unions ACAS Code No 2
Time Off for Trade Union Duties and Activities ACAS Code No 3
Code of Practice: Picketing, Department of Employment
Code of Practice: Closed Shop, Department of Employment

Glossary of legal terms

Act: A written law passed by both Houses of Parliament and signed by the Queen.

Additional award: A sum of money to compensate a successful unfair dismissal applicant for the failure of an employer to abide by the terms of a tribunal order of reinstatement or re-engagement.

Adjournment: Used in this handbook to cover the situation where a tribunal halts the hearing for a short period because of a problem which can be dealt with without putting the hearing off to another date.

Appeal: Right to take a legal case to a higher legal body on the grounds that the body hearing your case were mistaken on a point of law in finding against you.

Appellant: The person who appeals against a decision.

Applicant: The person who brings a case against another to an industrial tribunal.

Arbitration: Where an independent outsider listens to both parties in dispute and comes to a decision on their problem.

Associated employer: Two employers are associated if one is a company of which the other directly or indirectly has control or if both are companies of which a third person directly or indirectly has control.

Basic award: Sum of money for which successful unfair dismissal applicants may be eligible assessed on age and years of service.

Code: Document produced by official body such as ACAS to give guidance on the law and be taken into account in legal proceedings.

Common law: The law made directly by the courts themselves rather than law made by interpreting Acts of Parliament.

Compensatory award: Sum awarded in unfair dismissal cases to compensate for the actual loss suffered because of the sacking.

Conciliation: Attempt by outside third party to encourage those in dispute to come to their own agreement.

Consolidation: The power of industrial tribunals to consider two or more cases together because of common questions of law and fact and because similar remedies are being claimed.

Constructive dismissal: Where the tribunal accepts the argument that whilst an individual technically resigned, the employer's breach of contract which prompted the resignation means she or he was in reality dismissed.

Continuous employment: To qualify for most legal rights you will need to show that you have worked for your employer for a certain period with no breaks in continuity. The courts have developed special rules to decide whether these requirements are met.

Contract: Legally enforceable agreement written or verbal.

Contribution: Reduction of compensation in unfair dismissal cases by a certain percentage because of the view that the applicant's conduct was to that degree to blame for the dismissal.

Costs: Sum awarded by industrial tribunal against a party whose conduct is frivolous, vexatious or otherwise unreasonable.

Cross-examination: Right of either side at a tribunal hearing to question the other side's witnesses on the evidence that they have given.

Crown employment: Employment by a government department.

Damages: Compensation losing employer pays a worker in a legal case to place him or her in the position they would have been in had the wrongdoing not occurred.

Directions: Meeting between parties and chairperson, registrar or judge to discuss handling of the case.

Discovery of documents: Power of industrial tribunals to order either side to make available documents relevant to the case.

Dismissal: Sacking with or without notice or constructive dismissal.

Effective date of termination of employment: Date from which time limits for tribunal applications run. Also establishes period of continuous employment.

Employee: Somebody who works under a contract of employment or service as lawyers still call it.

Entry of appearance: Employer putting in his or her defence to your case usually by filling in IT3 and returning it within 14 days of receiving IT1.

Examination: The right of each party to question the witnesses they have called at the tribunal hearing.

Fixed term contract: Contract of employment which ends on a specific date and which cannot be ended by notice before that date.

Further and better particulars: Power of tribunals to issue an order against either party instructing them to provide more details of the grounds they rely on in their case and any relevant facts or arguments.

Hearsay evidence: Evidence imputed to a person not present at the hearing.

Independent contractor: Worker often self-employed who is employed on a contract to render services as opposed to an employee who works under a contract of service.

Interim relief: Method by which somebody allegedly dismissed or victimised for union membership or activities can submit a claim to a tribunal within 7 days and get a quick hearing before a tribunal chair who can declare the contract should continue and wages be paid until the full hearing.

Interlocutory matters: Issues such as further particulars or discovery of documents which you need to think about between application and hearing.

Jurisdiction: Whether tribunals have the legal right to hear a particular case.

Mitigation: The duty of an applicant to minimise the loss suffered because of the respondent's action. In unfair dismissal, for example, failure of the applicant to seek suitable alternative employment is taken into account by the tribunal in assessing compensation.

National Insurance tribunals: Quite separate bodies from industrial tribunals, they deal with your rights under the social security system which may arise at the same time as you are taking a case to an industrial tribunal.

Originating application: Written complaint to industrial tribunal to start your case – usually by filling in form IT1.

Postponement: Used in this book to cover situation where a case is put back to another day because for example one party fails to attend.

Pre-hearing assessment: Hearing held so that tribunals can assess doubtful cases or doubtful parts of cases and by indicating their opinion discourage parties from bringing or defending cases.

Preliminary hearing: To decide whether a tribunal has jurisdiction to hear a case.

Prescribed element: That part of the compensation the tribunal awards you from which any social security benefits that you have received can be recouped by the DE or DHSS.

Questions procedure: Method used to enable applicants and prospective applicants in race and sex discrimination cases to obtain more information about the alleged discriminatory act.

Recoupment: Claiming back from your boss or ex-boss by the DE/DHSS of social security benefits that you received.

Redundancy: Dismissal because the employer's need for employees to do work of a particular kind has ceased or diminished.

Re-examination: Right to re-question your witness after she or he has been cross-examined.

Respondent: The party against whom the case is brought, usually the employer.

Review: Rehearing of the case or some aspect of it because of some defect in original hearing.

Statute: See Act.

Statutory Instrument: Law passed by a minister, granted authority by Parliament.

Striking out: Ability of tribunal at any stage to order either side's case to be dismissed or amended on the grounds that it is scandalous, frivolous or vexatious or for want of prosecution – where either party is not following the case up.

Test case: Where the two sides *agree* to extend the decision in a particular case or group of cases to other cases where the facts and issues are similar. The decision in the test case is not *legally* binding as far as the other cases are concerned.

Time limits: Periods laid down in the relevant acts by which applications have to be made to industrial tribunals if the case is to be heard.

Week's pay: The minimum period you are entitled to under your contract, used as the basis for calculating pay for most of your statutory rights such as unfair dismissal and redundancy.

Witness order: Power of tribunal to require a person to attend a tribunal hearing to give evidence.

Worker: Person who works, normally works or seeks to work under a contract of employment or for a government department or as a self-employed person.

Written particulars of the contract of employment: Written details of your terms and conditions of employment which an employer is obliged to issue under the EP(C)A.

Written representation: Written evidence in substitution for oral testimony which, if it is to be admitted at the tribunal hearing should be submitted seven days before the hearing date.

Case index

Page references are given in bold type.

Index